Printed and bound in the UK by MPG Books Ltd, Bodmin

Published in the UK by SMT, an imprint of Sanctuary Publishing Limited, Sanctuary
House, 45-53 Sinclair Road, London W14 0NS, United Kingdom

www.sanctuarypublishing.com

ISBN: 1-84492-020-8

CRASH COURSE DJ

Tom Frederikse and Rob Cowan

smt

CONTENTS

WEEK 8   134

CD CONTENTS

1 Two Gather, 'Ambient Qat' (135bpm)

This tune becomes easily mixable when the bass drum enters at about 1:30.

2 White House, 'Come On In' (128bpm)

With an easy drum front, this one features big fills – especially at bar 16.

3 Acid Queens, 'Lonely G Dub' (129bpm)

The intro is slightly difficult here so better mix from the drum entrance at first.

4 B M Ex, 'The Other Side' (126bpm)

A floaty, ambient front which could be used as an 'FX' record.

5 Acid Queens, 'Ready' (131bpm)

This one features jamming jungle drums which can be easily mixed with anything.

6 BB Miles, 'Sunrise' (138bpm)

Such a static, ambient front as this is handy to float over a tune as an 'FX' record.

7 Mooly Rouge, 'Tribalism' (130bpm)

A standard bass-drum front with various drum entrances makes this easy to mix.

8 Will E Robbins, 'Mimaylian' (127bpm)

Virtually an all-drum tune until about 3:30 (the bass, when it appears, is really too low to be heard or get much in the way), this beat is easily mixable.

9 Abbagaveny, 'For Your Love (Instrumental)' (134bpm)

This is the instrumental mix of the tune, featuring plenty of musical cues to help you fit the vocal mix over it.

10 Abbagaveny, 'For Your Love (A Cappella)' (134bpm)

This vocal-only version ideally should start just after beat 2 in the first bar of the phrase.

ACKNOWLEDGEMENTS

THANKS TO...

- Rob, for being such a top geeza and doing what it takes (again). As always, you're a star... Wa'eva.

- Jules for helping with the tunes – yet again – and sorry about that lost credit for your fantastic music, man.

- Iain MacGregor for being a dude and believing in us, and Lewis Brangwyn for doing a smashing job of editing.

- Finally, and most importantly, this book is for Mish, Molly, Casey and Ruby – undoubtedly the best people in the world.

FOREWORD

The art of DJing has inspired generations of music and dance fans for years, and its

evolution continues at breakneck pace, with many more enthusiastic aspiring

turntablists lining up to learn the tricks that thousands of dancers thrill to in clubs

around the world. But DJing – like just about everything else – is an acquired skill. It

takes time to learn and, of course, every student needs guidance. That's where

Crash Course DJ fits in. Over the course of the book, you'll learn not only how to use

your turntable, but also what to put on it, how to perform tricks with it, and what

alternatives there are out there to the traditional vinyl-and-deck setup.

Once you've completed the eight week-long lessons, *Crash Course DJ* offers an

insight into how you might pursue a career as a DJ, touching on the practicalities of

the sharp business end of the stick, and how to make your profile as a DJ rise above

the rest. By the end of this book, you should have gained the necessary skills and

confidence to get out there and gig. Happy DJing!

INTRODUCTION

Followed properly, this book will teach you how to DJ very quickly, but the old rule

still applies: no pain, no gain. Whatever you do and however you do it, you still must

practise – a lot – to see any useful results.

Each of this book's eight 'weeks' provides an entire sub-world of DJing – and you

could easily spend a month in each if you choose to dig deeper. For those with the

inclination, it will provide a more comprehensive foundation for your DJing if you

were to take extra time for each week's topic to refer to other sources (such as by

going to a club to observe a DJ in action or by reading a book called *DJ Techniques*,

also available from SMT) for the bigger picture. For those who want the hard stuff,

want it fast and want it now, however, this book does exactly what it says on the tin.

With just an hour of practice each day (in addition to reading and following the

material in each day's lesson), an absolute beginner can become an impressive DJ in

just eight short weeks. Your daily hour of practice, however, needs uninterrupted

concentration, an enthusiastic attitude and – above all – determination and patience.

The road to DJ Heaven, though, is uneven – rocky in places, for even the best

students – and requires persistence. Don't be put off by lessons that may seem

impossible to understand at first or exercises that are difficult to perform. It's all

part of the plan when some skills are easier to master than others.

With regular practice and dedication to the daily and weekly plan, this *Crash Course*

will turn you into a DJ worthy of risp – and who would want to be anything else?

ABOUT THE BOOK

This book is an eight-week DJ course designed to take you step by step through the rudiments of becoming a successful DJ. Each week is broken down into daily lessons, and at the end of each week is a test designed to ensure you have all the basics under your belt. Each week looks at different aspects of DJing – from the equipment you'll need to how to get best out of it and taking in some of the tricks every good DJ knows. These lessons will vary in time to complete, although some will inevitably be more challenging than others, so don't get frustrated if you're unable to complete the lesson that day. Good DJing is not a skill you can learn overnight, so patience should be your watchword. Here's a key to what you'll come across over the eight weeks:

 Test – an opportunity to test your ability in order to apply material learned over the previous week.

 Quote For The Day – words of wisdom from renowned DJs.

 Thought For The Day – a nugget of information relating to the day's lesson.

WEEK 1

DAY 1: EQUIPMENT AND SETUP – TURNTABLES

- To understand the differences between various types of turntable.

- To understand the basic elements and functions of a turntable.

THEORY

The turntable is the DJ's main tool. It is the thing that

plays the records that will eventually be amplified

through the system. Turntables (or 'decks' – or 'record

players', as your dad might call them) are old

QUOTE FOR THE DAY

I have standards for what I use. I need to have Technics 1200s. – *Jes One*

technology; the first turntables appeared over 80 years ago and the basic idea

hasn't changed: a motorised platter spins the record underneath a tone arm with a

needle that tracks the record's grooves inwardly. The beauty lies in the simplicity.

There are only three wires hanging out of the back: the audio lead (the stereo audio

output, which is, technically, two wires because it has a left and a right); the power

lead (which plugs in to the wall); and the ground (or 'earth' – more on this later).

TURNTABLES

There are two main types of turntable: belt drive and direct drive. The direct-drive

version has a high-quality precision motor that directly spins the turntable platter.

There are, however, two kinds of direct-drive turntables: the electronic direct-drive

motor uses magnets and electric current to create the force required to spin the

platter, while the other kind of direct-drive motor is attached directly to the

turntable platter. The electronic direct drive is preferred because it has a smoother

performance. In the second type, when the motor is directly connected to the platter, the moving parts of the motor tend to cause some vibration and create rumble or distortion of the sound. Overall, however, the advantage of both types is that direct-drive decks are better suited for DJ use because the startup time is faster, the revolutions are more consistent, and there is more 'torque' (or turning power). More torque is better because it will rev up to speed faster and get back to speed more quickly after hands-on tricks, which will slow or even stop the platter. The only disadvantage is that the direct-drive turntable is more expensive.

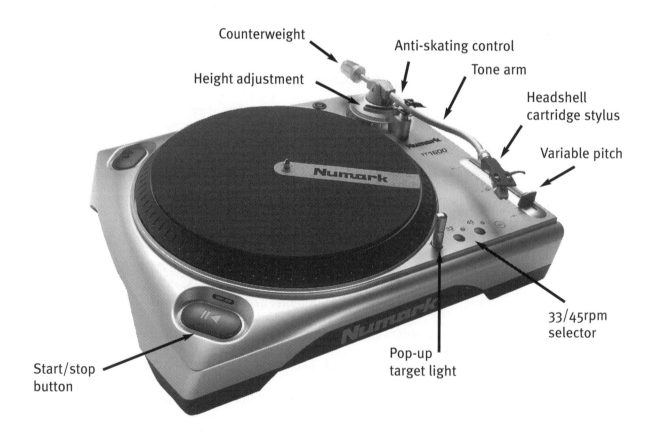

The standard controls found on a typical deck

The belt-drive turntable has a motor which turns a large rubber band-like belt to spin the turntable platter. The disadvantages of belt drive are that the belt eventually wears out, there is less torque (meaning slower start-up and recovery times) and the overall performance of the turntable becomes inconsistent as the belt wears out, which is made worse by the DJ aggressively cueing up records or scratching as the friction causes the belt to slip and eventually makes smooth spots on the drive belt. Worn-out belts also give the DJ less control over the records and can cause the platter to spin at uneven speeds.

WHICH DECK?

The 'King of Decks' – the Technics SL-1200 MK II – remains the turntable of choice for most DJs. Despite the competitors' many attempts to make comparable turntables that cost less or deliver better features, DJs overwhelmingly choose the old favourite. Recently, though, Vestax, a big player in the mixer scene, has performed well and does offer serious alternatives, such as the PDX-d3S MKII and PDX-2000. Numark is also a big player in the deck stakes. Regardless of manufacturer, however, few decks have more than just the essential controls: on/off, start/stop, speed (33 or 45rpm) and pitch control (for fine speed adjustment).

The speed of the motor in better-quality turntables will be controlled by a 'quartz-lock' mechanism through which the speed of the motor is constantly measured against a quartz crystal (similar to the mechanism in a watch). Some turntables feature a handy 'speed check' device in the form of the lighted dots or bumps on the side of the platter. When the platter is spinning properly at the indicated pitch, the line of dots appears to

remain still. (The 'platter', incidentally, is the round metal disc underneath the rubber or felt slipmat. It's usually silver, and if it's an expensive deck it will be made of aluminium, which doesn't warp. A low-cost turntable will use sheet metal.)

TONE ARM

The turntable's tone arm plays an important role in overall performance. A good, sturdy tone arm will keep away unwanted vibrations and, ideally, the counterweight (weighting of the tone arm) will be very precise and allow a wide-range of weights (from as little as half a gram to as much as five grams). If the weighting is not precise, sound quality may be unnecessarily lost when compensating for a bouncy floor or a heavy bass response.

A typical counterweight setup

TRACKING

'Tracking' – ie the way in which the needle rides in the record groove – can be controlled in three ways: via the anti-skating control (side-to-side movement); by using a counterweight (ie weighting the tone arm, increased by twisting the weight closer to the middle of the arm) and adjusting the height (ie controlling the downward angle of the needle – the higher the height, the greater the angle between the tone arm and the surface of the record; the more angle, the better the tracking because the needle digs deeper). Remember that all three adjustments work together, and when all three are set high, track ability is increased (but there is increased wear on the precious records).

To set the tone arm weight, start by letting the tone arm hang at the edge between its rest stand and the platter. Keep the weight screwed well up the tone arm and gradually adjust it until the tone arm hangs in the balance at the right height so that it just barely hits the record. This point is the 'zero' point and, if the scale doesn't already read it, set it to zero now. Then add more weight, according to the manufacturer's instructions (or even more for performing tricks and so on).

EXERCISE

For this introductory exercise, be sure to use an old crappy record that you don't care about (as you're likely to do some damage to it!). The aim of this task is to familiarise yourself with the correct adjustment of a typical tone arm.

Start by setting the weight to two grams and check to see that the needle tracks well (stays firmly in the groove). Experiment by setting the weight very lightly – to about

half a gram or less – and see at what weight the tracking gives out (the needle should quickly glide across the grooves, slightly damaging the record). Then, try setting the weight heavily and look closely at how the needle rides low down on the disc. Increase the weight by using the counterweight first, then try doing it by using a few small coins (for those desperate moments at a gig when the counterweight is stuck or broken).

THOUGHT FOR THE DAY

When using coins as a counterweight, it helps to stick them down somehow so that they don't fall off, so always remember to carry a couple of small coins and some double-sided sticky tape to stick them down with.

DAY 2: CD PLAYERS

TODAY'S GOALS

- To note the differences in DJing between turntables and CD players.

- To understand the basic functions of a CD player.

THEORY

While CD players in clubs were a rarity only a few years ago, they have become standard since specialised DJ models have become affordable. The main disadvantage of mixing CDs is that you can't physically see the music on the disc – unlike vinyl records, on which you can see the grooves as they are being played. While this initially presented a huge problem for the DJ, it was overcome by the modern DJ CD player, which enables you to pinpoint (or 'cue up') any specific spot on the CD as well as use speed control ('varispeed' or 'pitching') and even manipulate and cut up the disc much as a DJ would with a vinyl record.

QUOTE FOR THE DAY

CDs are decks that play plastic records with invisible grooves. – *DJ Rodman*

Most clubs offer two CD players in the booth and they will usually be set up as a 'double-console' version, with two players mounted together side by side. The stand-alone units are invariably better (although, of course, you'll then need two).

Unlike turntables, CD players boast quite a few controls. The basics are: on/off (power), start/stop (or play/pause) and rewind/fast forward (for leaps across the disc). Most models use the home version of rewind/fast forward, in which a long

hold of the button shoots to the beginning of the next (or previous) song and a short touch of the button moves the disc along only slightly. Every player is different and you'll need to practise with your controls to become adept.

The DJ CD player will also have a speed control for fine pitch adjustment (which works exactly as the turntable version) and at least three 'cue-point storage' buttons which enable you to 'remember' up to three different specific points on the CD. This is the most important feature of the DJ models in that the DJ is able to find the perfect spot on the CD for mixing (using the rewind/forward and start/stop buttons) and then 'spin it' into the mix at the right time (which, for vinyl, would be done by hand) and return to that spot over and over again. Of course, the stored cue points will be correct only for the CD that you are using at the time, and you will have to store new points for each new disc you load.

Pioneer CDJ-100S

Of course, the player will always have an eject button with which to remove the CD from the player. If the model has an electronic load system, it may be slow to open and close, which can be seriously annoying during a fast-paced set).

EXERCISE

Start by listening to a CD and choosing a spot at the beginning of a new section in the song that seems a good one for mixing. Use the start/stop button and the reverse/forward button (remembering to touch it lightly and briefly) to pause the disc at the chosen point. Now press and hold (for two seconds) the first cue-point button to store this spot on the disc. Check for success by playing the song from the beginning and hitting the first cue point at some point during the song at the beginning of a section or groove. The music should jump immediately to the previously chosen spot (and should sound impressive if the spot was well chosen and the finger action was timely).

THOUGHT FOR THE DAY

Some models can be tricky to load and unload, and it's always a good idea to get acquainted quickly with the loading of a new and unfamiliar model so that you don't waste crucial time putting CDs in and taking them out.

DJ

DAY 3: MIXERS

TODAY'S GOALS

- To get acquainted with the functions of a disco mixer.

- To understand the basic controls on a mixer.

THEORY

A mixer serves two purposes: pre-amplification and

level manipulation.

THOUGHT FOR THE DAY

What sort of DJ are you? You probably won't know

yet, but notice how important it is even at this

early stage.

Pre-amplification is needed because the signal of the

audio output of a turntable is so small. Every turntable

needs to have that weak signal boosted to a level that

can be handled by the other boxes down the chain, such as effects and power amps.

Pioneer DJM-300 DJ mixer

This 'pre-amplification' happens automatically, so you don't need to think about it, except to know that turntables must be plugged into Phono inputs on mixers (the other inputs – Tape, Mic and so on – won't have sufficient pre-amplification). So, yes, it is important to plug the various boxes into the correctly labelled sockets.

The other aspect of amplification that mixers provide is for headphones. All mixers have a tiny power amplifier inside them which is just strong enough to make a pair of DJ headphones audible over the din of the speakers.

A mixer is also the nerve centre for the DJ. It enables the DJ to mix the various sounds coming through the mixer on their way to the headphones and the speakers.

Mixers are divided into 'channels' and the most important controls are the channel faders, which enable you to introduce sounds from two or more of the various sources into the mix. Each channel fader corresponds to the source that is plugged into that channel: turntables 1 and 2 are usually plugged into channels 1 and 2 respectively, and those faders will therefore control the levels of each deck likewise. Further sources (usually CD players) will be controlled by channel faders 3 and 4.

In addition to a fader, each channel will have a 'trim' or 'volume' knob which controls the overall level of the source (usually set at about halfway up) and a 'phono/line' switch which switches between the sources in a channel and should be set appropriately for whatever source is plugged into that channel (the word *line* just means any source other than a turntable, such as a CD player).

Each channel will usually feature a PFL (Pre-Fade Listen) switch, which, when activated, will enable you to listen to only that channel in the headphones without affecting whatever sound is going out to the amps (and speakers). This is how the DJ is able to cue up the next record without the audience hearing what he's doing. Most mixers will feature an overall PFL 'level' knob to control the PFL volume in the headphones.

The key feature of a disco mixer is called the *crossfader*. This fader – usually situated across the top or the bottom of the mixer – enables you to fade between the channels which have a source playing in them with their channel faders up (if a channel fader is down, it cannot be heard regardless of where the crossfader is placed).

Most DJs will want a crossfader (or the bizarrely named *hamster switch*), which enables them to fade smoothly between channels. Note that 'turntablists' (or scratch DJs) will want a device that allows more intricate or faster moves.

All mixers will also have a master fader or level control to determine the overall volume of the system. Other handy – if unnecessary – features include VU meters (needles that jump to the music), lights (which shine to the music), beat counters (lights that flash during beat hits), 'kill switches' (which enable you to cut in and out certain frequencies or all of the sound) and tone controls (EQ).

EXERCISE

Play a record on each of your two decks and practise raising and lowering the

channel faders to hear how loud the level gets at different settings. Try to set an

equal level on each record and experiment with the crossfader to see at which point

both records can be heard and at which point only one record is distinguishable,

then try out the kill switches to understand how they depend on the settings of the

faders in order to have an effect.

THOUGHT FOR THE DAY

When choosing a mixer, choose the features that suit your style of DJing.

A turntablist will have different requirements from a beat mixer.

DAY 4: SPEAKERS AND AMPLIFIERS

TODAY'S GOALS

- To understand the interplay between speakers and amps.

- To understand the signal flow of audio.

THEORY

The signal that comes out of a disco mixer cannot be plugged directly into speakers because it's too weak. The master stereo outputs at the back of a mixer provide only a very tiny signal which must be amplified, using a power amplifier, before it can be turned into sound using a set of speakers. Power amplifiers will have very few connections at the back (just left and right sockets for 'input' and 'output') and even fewer controls at the front – usually just left volume and right volume (volume and level meaning the same thing here).

Most speakers can be described as being either 'two-way' or 'three-way', meaning that underneath the front grille cloth they actually have two or three individual speakers. The first kind has just a woofer for bass (low-pitched) sounds and a tweeter for treble (high-pitched) sounds, while three-way models have a third, mid-range speaker for the in-between sounds. This doesn't make the three-way speaker sound any better, necessarily; it simply enables the woofer and tweeter to specialise a bit more by letting the third speaker handle the middle bits. The most important factor that determines sound quality is the overall *combination* of speakers and amplifiers and the suitability of them for each other. Some speakers are even one-way models, although these often produce lo-fidelity sound.

Because the speakers are split in their duties (two or three ways), they need to be fed only the high or low (or middle) sounds as appropriate for their designated job. This splitting up of the sound is done by a device called – a tad confusingly – a *crossover*.

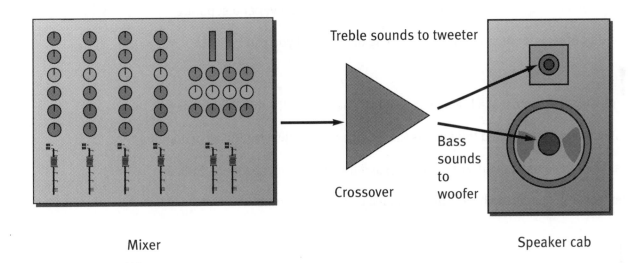

Mixer

Treble sounds to tweeter

Crossover

Bass sounds to woofer

Speaker cab

How a crossover works

Now we can put it all together: the signal comes out of the mixer and is plugged into the crossover, where it is split into bass and treble sounds. The bass-signal output of the crossover is then plugged into a large amplifier (because bass requires a lot more power) while the treble-signal output is plugged into a smaller amplifier. The amplifiers make the signals more powerful and the amps are plugged into the speakers (bass output into the bass speaker input, treble output into treble) and the speakers make the big sound.

DJ

In a large sound system, this setup will require one crossover box, two or three amplifiers and speakers with separate inputs at the back for bass, treble and – possibly – middle. In smaller rigs, the crossover may be incorporated inside a single amplifier and the speakers may be wired so that just one connection from the amplifier to the speaker is necessary. This may look like a simpler system, but it should be remembered that the same complex system of crossover and separate amps and speakers (for bass and treble) is going on – even if you can't see it.

For home practice purposes, a home amp and two speakers will suffice – and they don't need much complicated thinking as the manufacturers always hide all of it and you just need to connect the mixer to the amp and the amp to the speakers. Still, as a professional DJ, it helps to have a bit of an idea of how it all works.

EXERCISE

If you have a system with either separate amps or two-way speakers, try unplugging just the bass or treble speakers or amps and listen to the result. Notice that the music sounds very muffled or very thin. Recognising this result is helpful when troubleshooting technical problems at a gig.

THOUGHT FOR THE DAY

When wiring a system, keep like with like: tape together wires as audio left and right, or treble and treble, and so on. This will help you isolate problems if and when they later arise.

DAY 5: HEADPHONES, CARTRIDGES, SLIPMATS AND LEADS

TODAY'S GOALS

- To understand the functions of these accessories.

- To understand the basics of how to use them.

THEORY

Headphones are the easiest things to understand: they just need to be very sturdy and they need to enclose the ear completely in order to shut out the sound from the speakers. You might consider using a pair with a long lead so that you can dance around a bit while you're mixing. The most important part, however, is that the headphones should be durable – few DJs are able to make a pair last longer than a few months – as headphones tend to get dropped, stood upon, wet or crushed very quickly. Clearly, it makes no sense to spend more money than absolutely necessary.

The most important part of the turntable is the cartridge and the bit inside, called the *stylus*. The stylus tracks through the grooves of the record, riding over tiny bumps and indentations. These movements are converted into electrical signals inside the cartridge which are sent up the tone arm. There are two types of stylus: spherical and elliptical. The shape of the stylus determines the sound quality and tracking ability of the cartridge. In general, a spherical stylus will track better and provide for slightly less wear and is better suited for scratch DJs. An elliptical stylus has a better sound but is more likely to wear out records. Cartridges, in general, tend to wear quickly, so in the early days its not worth spending a lot.

DJ

The conventional common cartridge is installed by screwing it into the underside of the tone arm's headshell and then connecting the four wires to the four rods using an obvious colour-coded system. Do, however, be careful to screw the cartridge in straight so as not to cause extra wear on the records. There is also another kind of cartridge which comes ready to wear and is entirely hassle-free; just screw it straight into the headshell – no wires, no fuss.

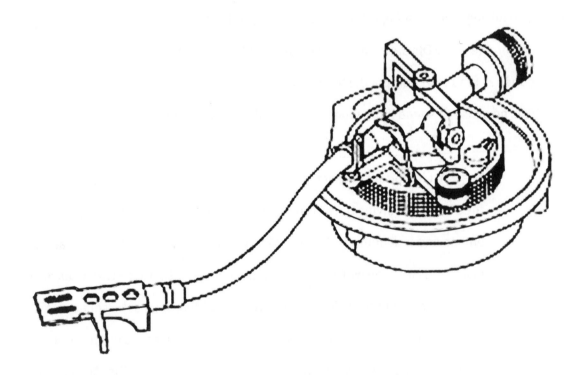

A typical tone arm

Slipmats are unnecessary when using domestic turntables because non-DJs don't want the record to slip. Proper DJing, however, requires that the record is able to move independently of the metal platter on top of which it sits, and this means you need something slippery on the platter. Slipmats are usually made of felt, although they could also be made of paper, cardboard or plastic. The slipmat should be thin and should easily turn on the platter and allow the record to turn on top of it – though, with the slightest pressure from your hand on the record, the platter, slipmat and record should turn as one.

The most popular type of slipmat is the decorated felt kind that you can pick up at almost any record store. They work well but tend to be expensive, so you might just as well go to a fabric store, buy some felt and make your own. You can also make them from the plastic sleeves from records (applying furniture polish to the platter is great for turntablists and scratch DJs, but just experiment and see what works for you).

Good-quality leads are the most underrated part of a rig. When you are costing out your system, don't forget to add extra money for decent leads. Ninety per cent of all troubleshooting ends up being a dodgy lead that either falls out of its socket (too old and loose or too cheaply made) or leads that simply fail inside the rubber casing (too cheaply made). Try to use thicker leads that have metal (brass, if possible) connectors, as these will rarely fail and tend to last much, much longer than the cheaper plastic varieties.

DJ

EXERCISE

Try disconnecting the cartridge from your tone arm and reconnecting it. While it is disconnected, study the small wire connections inside and try disconnecting and reconnecting them.

THOUGHT FOR THE DAY

A slipmat that isn't slipping enough may just be squeezing too tightly at the hole in the middle; try making the hole a bit bigger by carefully cutting it with a pair of scissors or a knife. When planning a system or a setup, measure how long the leads need to be and add a few extra feet to allow them to be run along edges or corners, where they will be under less strain and less likely to get caught or pulled on – and get a roll of gaffer tape to tape them there! Also, don't under-estimate the amount you'll have to spend on replacing the small items, as they break and wear out faster than most people think.

DAY 6: CONNECTING THE GEAR

TODAY'S GOALS

- To understand the signal flow of a sound system.

- To understand how the gear connects together.

THEORY

The sound starts in the grooves on the record and ends

up blasting your ear as it comes out of the speakers.

But what happens in between?

QUOTE FOR THE DAY

How important are the tools? It's the same way you wouldn't see a doctor performing a surgery with dirty hands or a dirty scalpel. – *DJ Rock Dee*

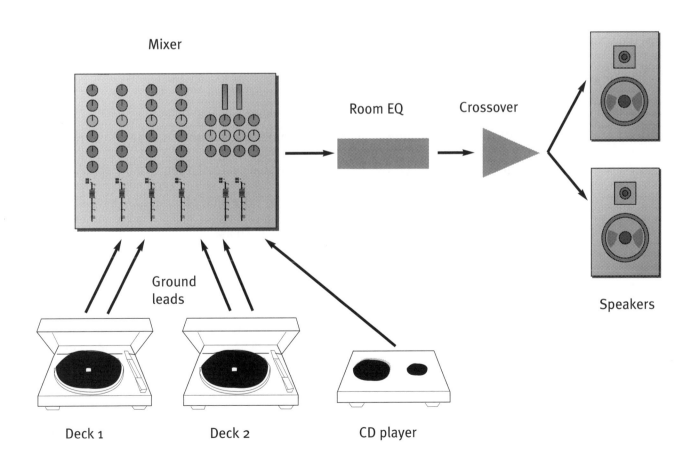

Mixer

Room EQ

Crossover

Speakers

Ground leads

Deck 1   Deck 2   CD player

The grooves on the record are a sort of physical code of the music. The stylus moves left and right and up and down and translates those movements into electrical current, which is sent through the four little wires in the cartridge and up the tone arm to the audio output wires at the back. These audio leads are connected to the phono input at the back of the mixer (or, for a CD player, to the CD or Line input). The mixer takes the signal and sends it – through the chosen channel fader and then the master fader – to the master stereo output sockets at the back of the mixer. The stereo audio output of the mixer is still a weak signal and needs to be connected to an amplifier to boost it, although the signal may go through a crossover on its way to the amplifier. The output of the amplifier is then connected to the speaker, which converts the electrical signal back into sound waves by actually moving the air in front of the speaker, just as your mouth moves the air in front of your head when you speak or sing.

That's it: the cartridge into the deck, into the mixer (then maybe into a crossover), into an amplifier (or two or three, if it's a big system), then into the speakers, and finally into your ear. There are a couple of extra bits, but these are extras which are not strictly necessary for the signal path, such as:

- The turntable ground lead. Turntables have a second wire hanging out of the back, in addition to the stereo audio output lead called the 'ground' or the 'earth', which must be connected to the 'ground' or 'earth' screw on the mixer. The turntable will work without this connection, but you will hear a loud and annoying low-frequency buzzing, which disappears when the ground connection is made.

- An overall room equaliser may be connected at a point just before the amplifier, enabling you to adjust the overall sound of the mix in the speakers, thus compensating for any acoustic problems that the venue may have. If this is present in the chain at all, it will have been put there by the club's technician and you needn't worry about its connections.

- Various effects may be connected to the mixer to enhance the sound or some part of it. Examples include delays, reverbs, equalisers, flangers, phasers and DJ multi-effect boxes.

 THOUGHT FOR THE DAY

If an overall room equaliser is used in your system or setup, keep it set to Bypass until you can listen to the system up and running. Then, engage the overall room equaliser only in order to solve specific acoustic problems, such as an overly boomy or a particularly muffled or tinny-sounding room.

EXERCISE

Identify each element of your system by placing it within the signal flow. Start by looking closely at the stylus and the wires connecting it to the cartridge. Follow the sound from the deck to the mixer. Examine your mixer closely and compare it to the electronic diagram of it in the owner's manual (if possible). Imagine the physical route that the signal takes inside the mixer, up through the channel fader, via the level knobs, and then through the master fader. Study the outputs at the back of the mixer and try to identify every output and say where it is intended to be connected. Follow the signal through your amp and speakers and try to spot where the crossover or equaliser might be. Identify all the different speakers within your speaker cabinet.

DJ

DAY 7

Now you've reached the end of the first week, it's time for your first test to make sure you're keeping up to speed.

TEST

1 What are the two main types of turntable?

2 Name three manufacturers of top DJ turntables.

3 What is tracking and what are the three ways to control it?

4 What is the name of the feature on a CD player that enables the DJ to return to a chosen spot?

5 What is a Phono/Line switch?

6 What are the two types of stylus?

7 Will a turntable work without its ground lead connected?

8 Where would a room equaliser be connected into the chain?

WEEK 2

DAY 8: DROP MIXING, BEATS, BARS AND I

TODAY'S GOALS

- To understand the basic divisions of music.
- To be able to count beats within a song.

THEORY

It may sound discouraging or off-putting, but music is very much like maths. Just as the number 64 can be thought of as four groups of 16 or eight groups of eight or 64 individual 1s, so a song can be broken down into various groups of individual *beats*. With most dance music (and especially house music), it's easy and instinctive to count the beats: in house music, the bass drum beats like a giant's heart on every beat as '1, 2, 3, 4'. Each beat is equal in length (duration) and the beats carry on relentlessly from beginning to end without ever speeding up or slowing down. A beat is the basic unit of music.

> **QUOTE FOR THE DAY**
>
> The beats of a song are like members of a team, all pulling together to achieve the same goal. – *Johannes Brahms*

It's important to remember that beats of music continue through the music at all times, regardless of whether the drums are playing or not; even during an ambient breakdown, the beats of the song carry on and must be counted, just as if the drums were still slamming away.

Beats come in two genders: front beats and back beats. The front beats are the first and third beats of each four, while the back beats are the second and fourth. The

...are the easiest to identify and lock onto (these are the beats that most

...e naturally clap on) and are almost always played by the snare drum. So the

classic drum beat of 'boom-crack-boom-crack' ('kick-snare-kick-snare') clearly sets

out the 1–2–3–4 beat pattern.

In all dance music (and in almost all Western music, for that matter), the beats are divided into *measures* (*bars*) which each contain four beats; this is why beats in music are usually counted as 1–2–3–4, without going higher in number. When counting the beats of a song, each grouping of four beats – ie each bar – should be felt so naturally that it's no longer necessary to think of beats individually; the listener's only thought should be of counting the number of bars that have passed. The beat and bar structure of music should be thought of as 'BOOM-crack-boom-crack, BOOM-crack-boom-crack' or 'ONE-two-three-four, ONE-two-three-four'. It might help to think in terms of beats melting into bars as letters melt into words.

 THOUGHT FOR THE DAY

Slower-tempo house music (about 118bpm) is the easiest to mix because it is relatively easy to follow the beat and bar structure: the bass drum hits on every beat and the crack of the snare on beats 2 and 4 is loud and easy to pick out.

EXERCISE

Listen to a dance record (ideally a house music tune) and try to identify the beat and bar structure. After you become comfortable counting the beats in each bar, try counting the bars as 'ONE-two-three-four, TWO-two-three-four, THREE-two-three-four, FOUR-two-three-four' and onwards. Try dropping the needle in the middle of a few different songs and see how long it takes you to orientate yourself with the records and identify the beat and bar structures. Try it with very different kinds of music and see how fast you can count the beats and bars. This process might take you much longer than a day to master, but it is crucial that you attain this skill.

DAY 9: BPM AND COMBINATIONS OF BEATS AND BARS

TODAY'S GOALS

- To understand the concept of tempo and bpm.

- To be able to count bars and phrases.

THEORY

The speed of a song, whether it is a fast song or a slow song, is known as its *tempo*, an Italian word meaning 'time'. In dance music, it's important to identify the tempo of a tune quite precisely, and a suitable system of measurement was devised for this purpose, which is why the term 'bpm' (beats per minute) was invented.

QUOTE FOR THE DAY

A musical phrase is just like a spoken sentence – it creates conversation.
– *Arnold Schoenberg*

It's actually so simple as to be almost stupid: you simply count the number of beats that go by during the space of one minute.

TYPICAL DRUM ARRANGEMENT IN 4/4 (ONE BAR)

Beats	1		2		3		4	
Bass drum	X	–	X	–	X	–	X	–
Snare drum	–		X		–		X	
Hi-hats	X	–	X	–	X	–	X	–	X	–	X	–	X	–	X

An X indicates where in the bar that instrument would sound.

When two songs share the same bpm, they will run at exactly the same tempo (speed) and can therefore easily be mixed together. This is the main premise behind most DJ mixing. So, if beats are 'letters' and bars are 'words' in the language of music, these musical words are strung together called phrases, which serve as the equivalent of sentences. A musical phrase is less strict than beats and bars, but it always exists nevertheless and can always be – and must be – identified in order to mix different records together cohesively.

As we saw yesterday, beats are bundled into groups of four to form measures, or bars. Similarly, bars are often tied into groups of eight bars to form a phrase. In dance music, bars are always – without exception – precisely four beats long and can therefore be easily counted. While phrases are not subject to such strict rules, we can, however, generalise for simplicity's sake (and this will be accurate for about 90 per cent of dance tunes); phrases are generally eight or 16 bars long, depending on tempo (slower tempos will usually mean a shorter number of bars in a phrase). The easiest way to identify the phrase structure of a song is to start from the beginning.

EXERCISE

Try figuring out the bpm of a song the 'hard way' by counting the beats for one minute. (It helps if you use a record that has the bpm marked on the cover so you can check your accuracy.) Next, try counting the beats and bars all the way through an entire song. See if you can identify, or 'feel', the phrases as they fall on the multiples of eight (ie 16, 32, 64, 96, 112, 128 and so on).

DAY 10: MUSICAL PHRASES

- To identify beginnings and ends of phrases.

- To identify similar phrases and suitable mix points.

THEORY

When you can easily count the beats in a song and identify the bars by quickly finding the correct position of '1–2–3–4' within a song, it's time for the difficult (and most important) bit: identifying phrases. As we saw, it's easiest to identify the beginnings and ends of phrases if you count from the very beginning of the song (and, therefore, know where the multiples of eight occur), but it's not always practical to play and count from the beginning; in fact, its damned inconvenient, and you'd think there must be a better way. Well, yes, there is.

There are almost always 'signposts' placed at the beginnings and ends of phrases which clearly flag them up. Here are a few indicators to look out for:

- Most phrases tend to have a cymbal crash at the beginning (on the first beat of the first bar of the phrase). Listen until you hear a cymbal crash and remember to count the crash beat itself as the first beat of the first bar at the beginning of the phrase.

- Many phrases feature a drum fill near the end of the phrase. Listen until you hear a drum fill (a busier drum pattern lasting about two, three or four beats); the first beat of the next bar (the start of the next bar) will be the beginning of the phrase.

- If there is a vocal on the record, the singer or rapper will often begin a sentence at the beginning of a musical phrase. The intonation or pitch of the vocal will often also rise at the beginning of the phrase. This is a crude indication, though, and it will rarely be right on the first beat, so – as you're always doing already, anyway – keep counting the bar structure to identify the first beat and bar of the phrase.

- Long sections without drums – or drum *breakdowns* – tend to be the length of a phrase. The top of the section will mark the beginning of the phrase.

These are only rough indicators, but they should go some way towards helping you to develop an instinct for identifying the beginnings and endings of phrases.

So, why is it important to locate the phrases so accurately? Because matching up records in order to mix them together requires aligning their phrases together. In other words, the object is to identify the beginnings of a phrases in each of two different records that have the same tempo (or bpm) so that they run together – alongside each other – as if two people were walking side by side at the same speed and with synchronised steps that start and end at the same time.

DJ

TWO PHRASES WHICH ARE TWO BEATS OUT OF SYNC

Record 1	1 2 3 4	2 2 3 4	3 2 3 4	4 2 3 4	5 2 3 4	6 2 3 4	7 2 3 4	8 2 3 4
Record 2	1 2 3 4	2 2 3 4	3 2 3 4	4 2 3 4	5 2 3 4	6 2 3 4	7 2 3 4	8 2 3 4

EXERCISE

Put two different records which are at the same tempo (or bpm) on the decks. One at

a time, listen to them and count the beats and bars, and identify the beginnings of

various phrases. Try choosing phrases in both records that sound similar and

remember where they are for use in another lesson in two days' time.

THOUGHT FOR THE DAY

Listen for big cymbal crashes – which usually play on the first beats of phrases

– in two different records to identify the points at which the records 'match up'.

DAY 11: DROP MIXING – HANDLING VINYL

- To feel comfortable handling vinyl.

- To be able to wind forwards and backwards.

THEORY

Your goal for this lesson is to lose any fear you may have of touching the intimate parts of a record. Start by picking up a piece of vinyl and looking closely at the grooves. Notice that it has lighter and darker bits. Of course, you know that the perfectly smooth and thin rings mark out the silences between the songs – that's how we find the beginnings of songs on a vinyl record. But this is a helpful hint: the smoother (and darker) bits are the quieter sections of a record, while the bumpy (and lighter) bits are the loudest sections.

QUOTE FOR THE DAY

You gotta put your hands on the music to feel the groove. – *Afrika Bambaataa*

The DJ should be able to 'read' the grooves of a record. If you're looking for an ambient breakdown in the middle of a record, the first step is to examine the vinyl for clues. Of course, if you can start with a visual prompt, you should.

Place the record on the deck and, without playing it, put your index finger on the label in the middle and turn the record with your finger. Try turning it as fast as you can and note how much pressure is needed to do this. Now try turning it as slowly and consistently as possible and note how much force you use.

Now the scary part: do the same thing again but place your finger (or fingers, if that's more comfortable) somewhere on the vinyl itself. Note how much more or less difficult it is to spin it. Try placing your finger at various places and move the record forward and backward. It might take some practice to be able to move the record as you want to without jerking the whole deck. Ideally, you need to practise handling the vinyl until you spin the record in every which way and speed without spilling an (imaginary) full-to-the-brim glass of water sitting on the label of the record.

When you're comfortable with your DJ hand on the vinyl, put the needle on the record (but without starting the deck spinning). Now turn up the volume a bit and listen to the sounds you can make by spinning the record forwards and backwards, fast and slow.

EXERCISE

Place the needle on the non-spinning record and try to spin it as quickly and as slowly as possible without making the needle jump. (This might take quite a bit of practice).

DAY 12: DROP MIXING – CUEING UP

TODAY'S GOALS

• To locate a chosen point on a record.

• To be able to cue up a record to a chosen point.

THEORY

Start this lesson by putting the needle on a record and finding the first beat of the tune. To do this, play the record from the very beginning and physically stop the record when you hear the first beat by placing your hand on the vinyl (on the opposite side of the record from the tone arm) and pulling it back slightly when you hear the first beat. The slipmat comes in very handy here by allowing the platter to spin underneath while you hold the record still on top. Hold the record still, against the force of the platter spinning underneath, and practise moving it slightly forwards and backwards. When you're comfortable with this

QUOTE FOR THE DAY

You have to walk before you can run, and walking for a DJ means learning to cue music. Cueing is starting a record's music at an exact point. You have to learn this so that you can drop the beat at a specific place. Cueing a song at its beginning is easiest. Set the needle on the record, spin the turntable clockwise until you hear a sound, stop, and back up a little. The point where the sound begins is your cue point. – *Q Bert*

feeling, try spinning the record anti-clockwise until you hear the backwards sounds stop entirely. This is this first beat of the record that you just passed. Now move your hand back into position (on the side opposite the tone arm). This is usually quite tricky for beginners as it needs to be done very quickly, and you might find it easier to buy yourself a bit of time by turning the record an extra half-revolution beyond the first beat so that, when making the move, the record can spin that much before hitting the tune.

DJ

Now confirm that you've still got the first beat cued up by moving (or 'scratching') the record slightly clockwise until you hear the sound of the first beat, and then back again to just before. (This creates the well-known *wucka-wucka* sound if done quickly and repeatedly.) All the while when doing this, you should watch the label of the record in order to find a reference point for that first beat. When you have identified the exact spot where the first beat is – and are actually able to 'touch' it by moving the record around to that spot and hearing the sound of the needle touching that beat as you scratch it – you will have successfully cued up a record.

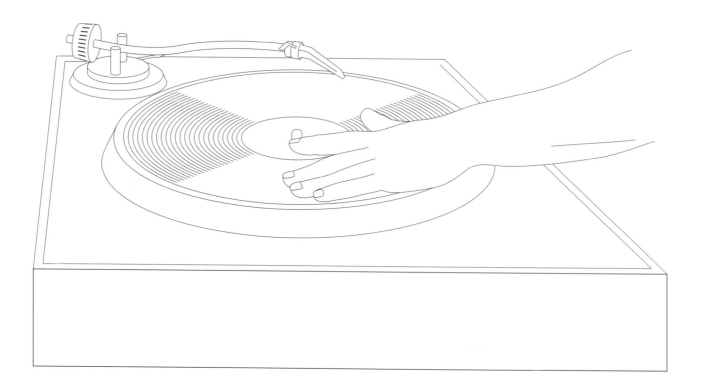

Cueing up a record

The next move is perhaps the most difficult skill that a new DJ must learn: you need to start the record spinning so that it hits the cue point (the first beat of the song, in this case) at the right speed and at the right time. The object is actually to feel the 'pull' of the motor as you scratch the record over that first beat so that you can judge how strongly to push the record quickly to get it up to speed. Give yourself a few extra inches before the cue point and try counting to four and then releasing the record, allowing it to move at the platter speed, and try to relax your hand at the same time. Of course, it will feel weird the first few times, and you'll need to do it a few dozen times before you gain any real control, but in time it will become second nature.

EXERCISE

Practise fast-forwarding and rewinding a record with your hand by pushing down hard enough to 'catch' the slipmat and gain control of the record and the platter. You'll find that you can push the record along quite fast without skipping the needle on the record because of the weight of the record and the platter.

DJ

DAY 13: DROP MIXING – THE CROSSFADER

- To handle the crossfader adeptly.

- To execute a crossfade.

THEORY

With your newly acquired skills in handling vinyl and cueing up, you are now ready to try your first drop mix. The idea is to bring in a record manually while fading another one out – without missing a beat. This is the seamless way to mix from one record to the next and is the first step in learning to beat mix.

Begin by cueing up the two records to the beginnings of phrases as you did on Day 5. It's probably easiest if Record 2 (the one you'll mix into) is cued to the first beat of the tune so that, when you mess it up the first 50 times, you can easily and quickly return to the cue point at the beginning of the record.

QUOTE FOR THE DAY

The crossfade was first accomplished by DJs using two separate controls, often rotary controls. They would maintain the volume in the room while fading from one record to another. It quickly became obvious that if a way could be found to fade with a single control, the task would be much easier.

– *Rick Jeffs,* DJ Times

The reason why yesterday's lesson on cueing up insisted that you learn to use just one hand is because you'll need the other to work the crossfader. Drop mixing is a two-handed affair: after cueing the record, getting it ready to fire by holding it just before the cue point, you'll need to split your thoughts and hands so as to shoot the record into motion while at the same time bringing the level of the new tune into the mix (which, through the magic of the crossfader, also brings the old tune out of the mix).

As should be clear by now, it is important to cue and re-cue Record 2 until you're sure you'll be able to release it at the right moment and get it up to speed before it hits the cue point. This is the most common task of the DJ and is what you're probably seeing when you watch a DJ in action with headphones on ears and hands on vinyl.

When we looked at the mixer in Week 1, we saw that the channel fader for each deck controls its volume in the mix, and you would be forgiven for wondering how you would move one channel up and another down at the same time smoothly. Well, of course, you don't: the trick is done using the crossfade, which 'overrides' the channel faders by keeping one channel out of the mix even when its channel fader is up. In this way, you can have two channel faders up at the same time and be able to hear either or both in the headphones, but with only one deck playing in the mix as you choose. The position of the crossfader determines which channel goes into the mix: if it's all the way to the left, only Channel 1 (and only Record 1) is heard in the mix; if it's all the way to the right, only Channel 2 is heard; if the crossfader is in the middle, both channels are live in the mix and both Record 1 and Record 2 will be heard in the mix at the same time.

DJ

After taking a few minutes to become acquainted with
how the crossfader works on your mixer, leave the
crossfader all the way on the left. Spin Record 1 from
about 20 seconds before the cue point, where you'll be
'mixing out' of it, while keeping Record 2 cued and
ready to fire under the fingers of your right hand. Now,
with your left hand, get ready to slide the crossfader all
the way across to the right: the aim is to have the
crossfader reach the right side at the exact moment

THOUGHT FOR THE DAY

A drop mix will sometimes sound better if you
move the crossfader across slowly instead of
quickly, but this is usually only true when the two
records are very similar in style, groove and
musical tonality.

that Record 1 hits its cue point while, at the same moment, Record 2 hits its cue
point. Perfectly performed, it should sound (in the speakers) as though Record 2 has
been seamlessly joined onto Record 1 with little or no jump in the beat.

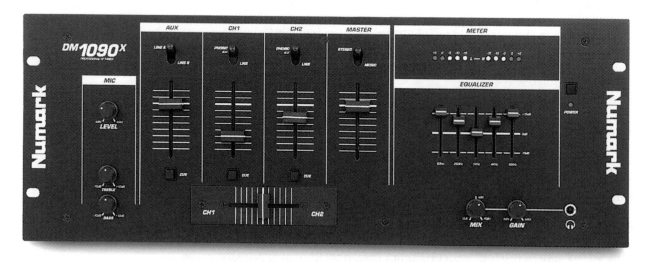

The crossfader all the way hard left selects Channel 2, and hard right selects Channel 3. With the crossfader centred, both channels are live. The crossfader enables fast and seamless segues from one selected channel to the other. Channel 1 cannot be affected by the crossfader on this model

In practice, of course, even the best DJs will occasionally choose to drop mix two records that do not share the same tempo, groove and vibe, but the whole idea of drop mixing is meant to cover the joins and minimise the disruption to the dancers. This is one reason why you've chosen beginnings and ends of phrases as cue points: the audience expects surprises and changes to the sound at these points. In fact, many classic records actually build in sudden shocks and changes to the music at beginnings of new phrases. In time, you'll develop a natural ability to adjust your drop-mixing technique for each record, in order to 'massage' the change-over point and make it sound like just one record, with no join at all.

EXERCISE

With records on both decks, leave the crossfader on the left and play both discs. Try switching between the records using the PFL monitor buttons so that you can hear one and the other in the headphones. Check that both records are at the same level by listening to the volume in the headphones and, if possible, by looking at the VU meters for each channel, one at a time. When both records are at the same volume, cue them to the cue points described above and practise drop mixing at the cue point.

Choose different cue points on different records, and this time don't choose the beginning of a song, but rather use points somewhere in the middle of each tune. When you're comfortable with that mix, try the same mix but with the crossfader moving slightly before and then slightly after the cue point and notice the effect: with some records it sounds brilliant, while with others it leaves an annoying gap or just doesn't seem to work at all.

DAY 14

Week 2's material has focused on the basic elements of music's structure and how the DJ uses them to mix using the crossfader. Take a look at the following test questions.

TEST

1   How many beats are in a bar of dance music?

2   How many bars usually make up one phrase in dance music?

3   Which beats in the bar are known as the back beats?

4   What does bpm stand for and what is it?

5   What function does the slipmat serve?

6   What is a crossfader?

7   What is drop mixing?

8   How can you visually check that both decks are playing at the same volume?

WEEK 3

DAY 15: BEATMIXING AND TEMPO

TODAY'S GOALS

- To better understand the concept of musical tempo.

- To understand relative tempos.

THEORY

By now we know that bpm stands for 'beats per minute' and that the word *tempo* means the speed of the music. Typically, modern dance music genres are defined by their tempos, and it helps, as a working DJ, to roughly know what is what.

QUOTE FOR THE DAY

No two records are precisely at exactly the same tempo, but sometimes they're pretty damn close. – *Anon*

BPM CHART

Reggae.................70–90bpm	Speed garage 125–140bpm
Streetsoul 80–105bpm	Hard house...........130–145bpm
Hip-hop.................85–110bpm	Techno 130–160bpm
Disco 105–120bpm	Trance 140–160bpm
Big beat 105–125bpm	Drum 'n' Bass 160–200bpm
Garage/house 120–135bpm	

The tempo of a song, however, is very rarely perfectly constant. Some records, especially older ones from before the '80s, will have varying tempos – sometimes quite wildly different – from one phrase to the next because during the recording process the tempo was being controlled by a human drummer playing live (who may have been out of his head at the time or was simply a crap timekeeper, even if the take 'felt' good), while some records will intentionally change the tempo during the song for artistic reasons. Modern dance records are generally more consistent in tempo because the music has been sequenced (ie composed, recorded and performed on or by a computer or a drum machine) and the computer can be programmed to perform at a perfectly constant speed.

But while modern dance records are usually close to it, there are reasons why absolute perfection is never actually found on a record. Even if the recording of a song is itself at a perfectly constant tempo, most turntables (being mechanical devices) are subject to tiny imperfections which can – even over just a couple of minutes – add up enough to cause a change in tempo that will throw off a perfect beat mix. In fact, even two copies of the same record are unlikely to run at the exact same tempo all the way through. For all these reasons, even when a DJ has perfectly beat matched two records, beat mixing will always require constant vigilance and speed correction.

Relative tempo refers to the comparison of two moving objects. Say you're driving down the motorway at 70mph and a car overtakes you. Clearly, that car is travelling faster than you are – but how much faster? One way to tell would be to increase your own speed until you'd caught up with him and then ease off until you were keeping

level – then your own speed would be the same as his and you could just look at your own speedometer. Another method, without you having to speed up at all, would be to judge the rate at which the other car passed you: did he ease past you? Did he whizz or fly past you very quickly? From this judgment, you can make an educated guess at his speed: obviously he is going faster than 70mph and it is unlikely to be as much as, say, 110mph – so now you only need to decide within those limits.

If that driver overtakes you quickly but then immediately encounters a police car, he is likely to slow down and he may fall back into pace with you so that your two cars are level again. But even if you and the other driver agree to drive at the same pace in adjacent lanes, keeping level with each other, it would still be impossible to stay exactly level at all times. You would need to watch each others' vehicle to see who is leading (or who is falling behind) and make constant adjustments accordingly. In this way, you can achieve very nearly the same speed – and pull close enough to stay apparently level. In music, then, when two songs are running at close to the same speed, they are said to have the same *relative tempo*.

THOUGHT FOR THE DAY

If you notice any glaring tempo shifts while listening to your (older) records, make a note of where they happen and keep the note in the sleeve for later reference if you should ever try to beat mix that record.

DJ

EXERCISE

Listen first to older records, especially disco records from the '70s, and then immediately to newer dance records from the '90s and try to hear the slight changes in tempo that will be more evident in the former. Try to notice the 'push-and-pull' feel of the live performance in the older record and contrast that with the 'machine feel' of the newer record.

DAY 16: SLOWING DOWN AND SPEEDING UP A RECORD

TODAY'S GOALS

- To become familiar with handling the pitch control.

- To control a record's speed manually.

THEORY

The aim of beat mixing is to keep two records running at the same speed, and this requires you to perform constant adjustments. There are two ways to slow a record or speed it up: manually (physically, with your hands) and by using the pitch control (the 'varispeed').

THOUGHT FOR THE DAY

The turntable and the records are there to be messed with. Don't be too respectful!

MANUAL METHODS

To slow down the record, brush your finger against the side of the record platter for an instant. The more pressure applied or the longer you keep your finger touching it, the more the record will be slowed. Alternatively, you can slow down the record by squeezing the spindle at the centre of the platter. This technique is more subtle and is often used as a refining adjustment after the initial adjustment has been made.

To speed up the record, put your finger on the label of the record and push down hard enough to 'catch' the slipmat so that when you then spin the record faster, it drags the platter itself along as well. Remember to spin the record clockwise (because you want to speed it up) and maintain enough pressure to move the platter under the record, as this will ensure that the needle doesn't jump.

Centre spindle

Pitch control

A record can be slowed by squeezing the centre spindle

Alternatively, you can speed up the record by gripping the spindle between your thumb and forefinger and spinning it faster than it is already going. This is a subtle method as it is quite hard to grip the spindle with enough pressure to spin it faster than it's already spinning. Of course, yet another method is to spin the record itself onwards without applying enough pressure to dislodge the slipmat, although this method often spins the record too far forward and has the added danger of causing the needle to jump.

PITCH-CONTROL METHODS

While it might seem easy at first glance, the varispeed is actually a difficult beast to master – especially as these pitch-control sliders will perform differently on different turntables. The boundaries are clearly set out on the slider: the middle position is the zero position, meaning no adjustment of pitch (so, theoretically, the speed should be exactly 33 or 45rpm), while the all-the-way-up position (as much as eight per cent) substantially and noticeably increases the speed and the all-the-way-down position (as much as minus eight per cent) similarly decreases it.

The difficulty with varispeeds lies in the middle ground. You will need to practise with your deck to discover how much effect the pitch control has when it is, say, above the middle position, and so on. One other difficulty may be in learning how fast the varispeed operates – ie how long after an adjustment does the pitch change? While this is always going to be quite a fast reaction time, small gradations will matter and you'll need hands-on experience to learn your decks.

EXERCISE

Put a record on the deck and practise these techniques with the sound turned up (a little) in order to hear just how much effect you're having on the speed.

DAY 17: SYNCHRONISATION AND BEAT MATCHING

TODAY'S GOALS

- To make two records run in time.

- To keep them running in time for an entire song.

THEORY

Start by putting two copies of the same record on the decks (as they will run at virtually the same tempo). Make sure both decks' pitch controls are set to zero. Use your well-versed drop-mixing technique (mastered in last week's lessons) to set Record 2 running so that its first beat coincides with the first beat of a phrase in

THOUGHT FOR THE DAY

Beat mixing is like guessing which train is moving when you're looking out of the train window and a train pulls out.

Record 1. If you have been precise in your drop mixing (and since both records have the same tempo), they should match well enough to run together in time for at least a few bars. If and when they don't sit exactly together in tempo, you'll need to adjust one record – by slightly speeding it up or fractionally slowing it down – to correct the tempo discrepancy. But before you can use your speeding-up/slowing-down techniques, you'll need to decide which record to adjust and how. Beware: this can be a confusing and frustrating game!

The trick is to listen to both records at the same time but always to keep Record 1 fixed in your mind as a reference point. Try to 'feel' Record 1 deep inside you without thinking about it too much by dancing or moving your lower body in time to it. Then, as soon as Record 2 hits the top of its incoming phrase, decide whether it has begun

slightly ahead or slightly behind Record 1 and then whether it's racing ahead

slightly or whether it's dragging Record 1 and falling behind. For certain genres of

music, you can choose specific elements to listen out for which tend to be dead

giveaways; in house music, for example, the relentless bass drum on every beat is

distinctive and easy to follow, while the hi-hat cymbal tends to play 16 times in each

bar, relentlessly, and so, by playing such short and fast notes, may tell the tempo

story even more quickly than the bass drum. In disco music, for another example,

the hi-hat tends to play the high-frequency 'peasoup, peasoup' pattern four times in

every bar and is often very loud and easy to hear.

Once you've plumped for one or the other record going faster or slower, you'll need

to make the counter-adjustment on Record 2 (or the record that isn't playing in the

mix yet, so that the correction cannot be heard by the audience), and only once the

correction has been made should you consider crossfading to Record 2 (at an

upcoming suitable moment). If you find yourself dithering about which record is out

of time, a surefire way of finding out is simply to slow down or speed up one of them

just a little bit. This will make the situation either better or worse and should quickly

reveal the problem.

DJ

When you've synchronised the two records, you can continue to refine the speeds, and at some point you'll find that they're running together so perfectly that they start to create an alien-like sound quality (when heard together, with the crossfader in the middle or in headphones). This effect is called *phasing* – more about this later.

After you've become adept with the two copies of the same record, try beat mixing with two different records – though the two records will need to be quite close in tempo if you're to have any hope of running them together with fine adjustments. With two different records, the initial adjustments are going to have to be made with the varispeed. Use the same principles to guess which record is going too fast or slow and make first large and then gradually smaller adjustments to the varispeed.

The idea is to over-compensate continually for each variation in speed – eg if you speed up a record, you'll have to wait for it catch up and overtake the other before slowing it down (by a smaller amount this time). When it falls behind again, speed it up again and repeat until you have 'zeroed in' on the correct pitch control setting.

You can gauge how much Record 2 is too slow or too fast by how big a manual adjustment is needed to catch up with Record 1. For example, if Record 2 can be pushed to catch up with Record 1 by fast-winding the spindle every two bars, it will need a varispeed adjustment of somewhere between two per cent and four per cent.

EXERCISE

Follow the directions for beat mixing two copies of the same record before

graduating onto two different (although similar-tempo) records.

With practice, it becomes possible to beat mix with only the varispeed and

without any manual adjustments at all. This requires very vigorous use of the

pitch control, such as jerking it up and down abruptly and briefly to over-

compensate continually in both directions by decreasing amounts alternately. For

example, to achieve a speed-up of just two per cent, you might move the

varispeed to six per cent very briefly just to 'rush' the record forward to catch up

and then swiftly return the control to two per cent.

DAY 18: PHRASE MATCHING

TODAY'S GOALS

- To know the criteria for choosing beat-mixable passages.

- To develop an instinct for 'spotting' compatible phrases.

THEORY

The aim of beat mixing is to have two records that can be made to 'work together' – ie they sound good when playing at the same time over the speakers. If you wish only to mix out of one tune and into another, without overlapping them, then a drop mix is the appropriate technique. So, since beat mixing is all about letting the two records play over one another (for a few seconds as a 'link' or, indeed, for several minutes as a 'new' record), it's crucial that the records have certain qualities that complement each other and don't have qualities that clash inappropriately.

Any two records, chosen randomly, stand only a small chance of having even short passages that would be compatible, while they have a strong likelihood of sounding entirely horrible when joined in musical matrimony. So what are the criteria?

1 The two tunes' tempos must be reasonably similar, with a difference of 5bpm or less.

2 The easiest phrases to beat mix together will be two sections of tunes that feature only drums. If both of the two drum patterns are especially complex or busy, the result might be a bit of a mess, so in general try to stick to relatively simple drum-based phrases while you're in the early learning stages.

3 If you do choose to mix passages with full instrumentation (more than just drums), bear in mind that different keys of music tend to clash horribly, especially if one of them is just slightly out of tune with the other.

4 If you choose two full vocal tunes, try to avoid playing the vocal passages together, as in 99 per cent of cases this will set the dog howling. If you play just one vocal, try not to bring it in mid-way through a line or phrase; try to wait for gaps in the vocal.

5 Big, fat, prominent bass lines, even when in the same key and in tune, tend to bulk up the mix too much and make everything sound ploddy and overly boomy.

EXERCISE

Try dropping your needle randomly on records and guessing which two phrases might work together, then try them in a beat mix. Look through your collection and imagine compatible phrases, then try them to see if you imagined them correctly.

THOUGHT FOR THE DAY

You can actually see where a breakdown section happens on a record. Look for the darker bits where the grooves seem more densely packed. This can be helpful when beat mixing to know when a section changeover is coming as a convenient and good-sounding point to mix or beat mix into the next record.

DJ

DAY 19: EXTREME RANGES OF PITCH SHIFTING

TODAY'S GOALS

- To become aware of the limits of pitch shifting.

- To consider the possibilities of the extreme ranges of pitch shifting.

THEORY

While it is very difficult to beat mix a tune at 108bpm with a tune at 125bpm, it's not impossible. We saw that most pitch controls have a range of up to plus or minus eight per cent, and this means that the maximum range – by setting one deck to its maximum and the other to its minimum – will be 16 per cent. For records with tempos of between 100bpm and 140bpm, this means the largest possible adjustment will be about 16–20bpm. So, theoretically, records of 108bpm and 125bpm could be beat matched.

If you were simply to put such widely spaced records on the decks and, without any pre-planning, try to beat mix, you would spend quite a lot of time in the initial 'rough matching' stage. So, to achieve such a radical connection in a reasonable time, you'll need to start by estimating the spread.

Many dance records will have the song's bpm printed on the sleeve or the label. Subtract the smaller number from the larger number to get the bpm spread of your chosen tunes and use that number as the starting point for the beat mix. For example, if one tune is 115bpm and the other is 129, then the spread is 14 and you should begin by setting the faster record at minus seven per cent and the slower

68

record at plus seven per cent. From this point, you can proceed with the beat-mixing technique as normal.

Of course, there is a far higher probability that a mix of such radically pitch-shifted records will sound terrible. After all, one record is playing much slower than intended (and probably sounds like a bad Darth Vader impression) while the other is playing far faster than intended (Mickey Mouse). But, on the other hand, there is always that slim chance that it will sound fantastic and make your name as a ground-breaking DJ...

EXERCISE

Try out a few far-fetched ideas with records of different tempos.

THOUGHT FOR THE DAY

When choosing records of quite varied tempos, try not to have other difficult factors at the same time; it's unlikely that a record of 108bpm will mix with a record of 123bpm if the records are in very different keys and have full vocals as well.

DAY 20: PHRASE MATCHING

- To come out of the mix smoothly.

- To consider factors that make a mix sound smooth.

THEORY

We've seen how to beat match and then beatmix two records, but the 'raw technique' is not all there is to it. The point, after all, is to move smoothly from one record to the next, always sounding natural and – hopefully – groovy and entertaining, as well.

We know that most dance records are divided into eight-bar phrases, but it's impossible to do smooth mixes of fewer than eight bars because you need the extra time to set up the moves. (These eight bars, referred to here, are not just the time that the records play together, but the total time the records play together in the mix.) And we've seen that the beginnings of phrases are the best places to mix in and out because this is where the listeners expect to hear changes anyway.

At this early stage of your beatmixing career, practise holding tunes in the mix for eight, 16 and then 32 bars, always making sure that you're able to drop out one of them smoothly at the end of the section. Use the crossfader to mix in the second tune over the first (remember to bring the crossfader to the middle while both records are intended to be heard) and then mix out again at the end by throwing the crossfader to one side or the other, depending on which tune you want to leave on until the next mix.

When mixing in and out this way, don't worry too much about being careful with the crossfader: the new tune will hardly be heard if the crossfader is only a couple of millimetres from one side. You need to develop the ability to 'throw' the crossfader from one side to the middle quite quickly. (In fact, on a scratch DJ mixer, the crossfader doesn't fade at all; it just switches from one side to the other at the middle point.)

On most dance records, there is a drum intro at the front before the main section begins, so take advantage of this by using the main section start point (or, more likely, eight bars before that point) as a cue point at which to mix in – after all, this is probably why it's there in the first place. This intro can also be used, when mixing out, as a buffer between big music sections by mixing into the drum intro section 16 or 32 bars before the main (musical) section hits. Mostly, these drum sections are so long as to allow you at least 32 bars to beat match your records, in addition to the next 32 bars of drums that lead into the main section.

So, once you've mixed in and things are going well, where do you mix out? Well, the best way to know where to mix out is to know your records so well that you can predict where the appropriate bits will come and, therefore, plan your mix properly by deciding ahead of time which bits are most likely to work best with others.

EXERCISE

When you're able to beatmix one record after another, practise keeping a mix going for five and then ten records, holding each pair in the mix for up to 32 bars.

DJ

DAY 21

WEEK 3 TEST

Week 3 has explained how the speed of music is measured and how you can use this knowledge when beatmixing.

TEST

1   Name a relatively slow and a relative quick genre of music.

2   Why are older records not at near-constant speeds while modern records generally are?

3   Name two ways of changing the speed of a record while it's playing.

4   Why is it important (whenever possible) to adjust the speed of only the record playing in the headphones and not the one in the mix?

5   How close in tempo must two records be in order to be considered 'reasonably close'?

6   Where is the best point in a record to mix?

WEEK 4

DAY 22: EQ, TONE AND LEVELS

- To understand the concept of sound waves.
- To understand the basic function of EQ.

THEORY

Sound moves through the air in much the same fashion as water moves in the ocean (the main difference being that you can't see sound). It's easier to understand sound if you think of it in this way.

THOUGHT FOR THE DAY

You don't need to understand the theory fully, but it helps to recognise the words at least.

Sound travels through the air as waves. Some sound waves are big (often as big as three meters long) and some are small (less than one centimetre). Sound waves travel by 'swimming' through the air in an alternating up-and-down motion. When a wave completes one full up-and-down movement during its journey through the air (like speech from someone's mouth to someone else's ear), the size of the wave is determined by the length of that full cycle of movement. The size of a wave – more commonly thought of as its length – is determined by its *frequency*. High-pitched sounds (which are small and short-cycled waves) are high-frequency sounds and low-pitched sounds (which are big waves with long cycles) have low frequencies.

DJ

Human ears can hear a wide range of frequencies, from the low rumble of a factory turbine to the high (nearly dogs-only) whine of a faulty electrical appliance or an old television. In numbers, the full audio frequency spectrum ranges from 20 cycles per second (Hertz or Hz) to 20,000Hz, though these numbers are the absolute limits of hearing, and in practice sounds rarely, if ever, occur at these extremes. As a more practical example, a bass drum will use the low frequencies of about 50–200Hz, a human voice will occur at around 800–2,000Hz (or 2kHz) and a flute will be heard as high frequencies of about 2–15kHz.

The function of an equaliser (an 'EQ') is to add or subtract parts of a sound either to cure some problem (such as to remove a high-frequency background hiss) or to make a signal sound different in some way (such as to give human speech more clarity or to make it more understandable on a telephone line). An EQ has one set of controls that enables you to choose the frequencies which are to be affected (such as 'low', 'mid' and 'high' – or, in other words the frequencies they relate to: 100Hz, 1kHz and 10kHz, respectively) and another set of controls that either adds to or subtracts from the chosen frequencies.

For example, an EQ could be used to remove the low-pitched rumbling noise from a recording of someone speaking in a factory, while it could also be used to add more high-pitched clarity to an old and muffled recording of a person singing.

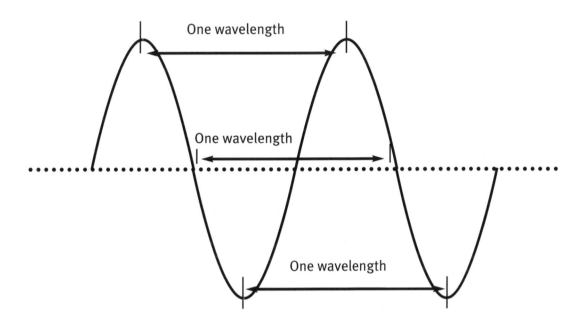

Sound represented as wavelengths

DJ

DAY 23: EQUALISERS

TODAY'S GOALS

- To understand which types of EQ are available.

- To understand what the various types of EQ can do.

THEORY

There are two basic types of EQ: graphic and parametric. A graphic EQ is the type most often encountered on mixers and amps, while a parametric EQ is a more specialised and powerful tool and is used primarily by professionals.

The graphic EQ such as the one illustrated overleaf has only the two basic functions: choice of frequency and cut/boost. The frequency control will determine the frequency which is to be affected. Most often, this choice of possible frequencies to affect is made for you insofar as the manufacturer has chosen the possible frequencies by providing one control for treble (or high-pitched frequencies or 'high end') and one control for bass (or low-pitched frequencies or 'low end'). Occasionally, you may see a more extensive choice which could include mid (or middle-pitched frequencies or 'mid range') and maybe even low mid or high mid. On more expensive dedicated EQ boxes there will often be a huge choice of over 30 set frequencies to choose from, set out on tiny sliders with labels ranging from about 50Hz to about 18kHz.

THOUGHT FOR THE DAY

An EQ can just as easily improve the sound of a room just ruin it.

The other function – cut/boost – is controlled by adjusting the same knobs (or *pots*) that are labelled for the chosen frequency: the pot labelled 'treble', for instance, is in its zero position when it's in the middle, so if it's left untouched then there is no effect on the treble frequencies. If that pot was to be turned clockwise, however, then the level of the treble frequencies would be boosted by some amount (the sound would be brighter) and if the pot was turned anti-clockwise, the treble frequencies would be cut and the resulting sound would be darker or more muffled.

A parametric EQ is just a more complicated version of the same thing. It has the same two functions but it has a third as well, called a 'Q adjustment', which adjusts the width of the basic frequency area that is intended to be cut or boosted. In other words, a parametric EQ can adjust either a very large chunk of frequencies as a broad-brush adjustment or it could adjust a very thin sliver of frequencies, and so is often used to remove feedback at a live gig without giving an overall muddy sound to the mix. So, a parametric EQ is rather like a precision weapon which can 'bomb' a specific target frequency without damaging (or affecting) the frequencies near that frequency.

Peavey Q1311 31-band graphic EQ

DJ

DAY 24: USING EQ FOR SOUND QUALITY

- To understand the capabilities of EQ.

- To know how to approach a pre-installed club EQ.

THEORY

The art of using an EQ is hardly more difficult than listening closely to music and sound. If you are told that a room has an exaggerated response to the frequency of, say, 100Hz (thereby making the music sound overly 'boomy'), then it's not so difficult to make the necessary adjustment on your EQ by turning down the 'bass' or the '100Hz' pot a little bit. Alternatively, if you're told a room sounds 'brittle' or 'cold', or that the room tends to make the frequency of 2kHz stick out too much, then it's no amazing trick to turn down the 'mid-range' (or '2kHz') pot. But it's a different story altogether when you're faced with a room that somehow doesn't sound as good as you know it could when there's no way to be certain of the exact problem. The only option in this case is to listen and make an educated guess.

THOUGHT FOR THE DAY

Remember to check different volumes and notice how the sound changes – louder settings usually have more low bass and high treble.

There are a few benchmark rules that you can generally rely on when trying to analyse a room:

1   Use a reference record. Put on a record that you know very, very well. Some

people carry a certain record to every gig they ever do in order to use it as a

reference. Listen to yours many times and in as many locations as possible.

When your reference record sounds particularly good, try to identify what it is

that appeals to you. Does the kick drum hit your chest in a certain pleasurable

way? Does the voice (or guitar or cowbell or whatever) sing out loudly over the

other instruments? Is there a certain high-pitched sound that is easily

discernable, such as a hi-hat cymbal or a shaker or a maraca or a tambourine or

whatever? If necessary, write down what you hear and any comments that you

think are relevant – and carry them with you. Likewise, when the record sounds

bad in a certain situation, try to identify what it is that sounds bad and why.

2   Move around the room. It's crucial to remember that there is no single spot

within a room that will accurately represent the whole room. The corners of a

room are notorious for trapping bass, a phenomenon in which the bass sounds

bounce back and forth between two close and adjacent walls (such as in corners),

causing the music to sound very boomy. The middle of a room is likely to sound

better than the edges (maybe only because the speakers are facing out towards

the middle). The closer you stand to a speaker, the louder and more direct (and

probably clearer and brighter) the sound. The only solution is to put on your

reference record and spend a minute or two in each of several locations trying to

compare the changes. It's not easy, but there's no other way.

3   Look at the speakers. If the sound isn't up to scratch, then, if practical, start by changing the position of a speaker or two before messing with any EQ. Of course, speakers are usually bolted down or are simply too heavy to shift or too big to place anywhere else, and this means EQ is the only possibility. But, where possible, think about the positioning of the speakers and experiment with different configurations. If you do change the positions – ie to aim them away from walls or toward the middle, etc – don't forget that you'll need to begin your listening experiment all over again afterwards, because speaker position is so fundamental that everything changes as a result of a move and you must restart your analysis.

4   Remember the 'human body effect'. A room full of people sounds very different from an empty room, and bodies tend to absorb sounds unevenly. If the dancefloor is large and flat, the crowd usually makes the sound more bassy, while uneven floors or rooms with corners tend to make the music sound tinny. The best way to deal with this is by comparing the sound early in the evening with the sound when the room is full at midnight. Obviously, you can only do this in a club that you visit often, but you'll develop an opinion over time. When trying to analyse a new room before your set, the only option is to guess – and it's usually a good rule of thumb that a sizeable club's dancefloor will get more boomy or bassy when full. Try to take this into account when listening carefully.

Once you've formed an opinion of how a room sounds, make a ruthless decision as to whether it's worth even trying to adjust anything. Consider what sort of EQ

options you have (is the club's room EQ any good?) and, most importantly, whether

or not the problems you noticed are actually bad enough to worry about.

If you have the chance and you *do* decide to have a go, start by sticking to

adjustments of just the rough areas of bass, mid and treble. Make a small

adjustment (3dB or less) to one of these and then go back on the floor and listen to

the same record again. If the problem persists, try making further small adjustments

and return to the floor to listen between every move. As a golden rule, if you make a

few small adjustments – or one or two large adjustments – and the sound doesn't

seem to be getting noticeably better, return to original position. And the only sure

way to be able to go backwards is to know where you started, so – before you adjust

any EQ, ever, at all – always make a note of where the controls were and write the

levels down. If you have no pen and paper, or if you can't see the pots properly to

note and remember their positions, you're better off not touching them and not

risking making the problem even worse.

EXERCISE

Think about the records in your collection that you know best and have known

longest and choose one as reference record. Listen to it on as many different

speakers and systems as you can and try to analyse the sound as described above.

DAY 25: HI-PASS AND LO-PASS FILTERS

TODAY'S GOALS

• To understand what EQ filters are.

• To learn their musical uses and how to use them to change the quality of a sound.

THEORY

Hi-pass and lo-pass filters (or HPFs and LPFs) are tiny, self-contained EQ boxes that can affect a sound hugely with just one seemingly small adjustment. The trickiest part is to remember that an HPF affects the low-frequency sounds and an LPF affects high frequencies. This is because an HPF cuts away the low sounds and lets the high frequencies pass unaffected, while an LPF cuts away the high sounds and allows the low frequencies to pass. It's confusing, but you'll get used to it.

The most common use of these filters is to use an HPF to stop low-frequency feedback. There are often times when a room is so boomy and the speakers so big that the system emits a huge, annoying and sometimes painful hum, like a foghorn, whenever it's turned up loud. This occurs because the system – the combination of the room and the positioning and the type of equipment – has an exaggerated response to a certain low-end frequency, and the solution is to use EQ to cut that low frequency out, which should maintain the loud volume but without incurring feedback. The actual frequency that's feeding back is very difficult to pinpoint, so the quick and easy solution is to execute an overall low-frequency cut on all low-end sounds, and this is what HPFs do.

HPFs have pre-selected hard-wired frequencies (usually at about 60Hz), so the only

adjustment you can make is to the level, and most HPFs only have a cut function but

no boost, so as you turn them up (or, more accurately, down), the bass sound starts

to disappear. Naturally, you don't want too much bass to disappear – only the

minimum amount necessary to cure the problem – so turn the knob very slowly and

then try turning the overall volume up again to make sure that the feedback has

gone away. If it has, stop there, but if not, increase the HPF amount a bit more until it

does. Always check to make sure that you've used only the minimum amount of HPF

to ensure that your bass sound is as loud as possible without incurring feedback.

Filters can also be used creatively, but we'll see about that later.

THOUGHT FOR THE DAY

Saying the term 'hi-pass filter' with extra stress on the middle word (as hi-*pass* filter) will help you to remember that it lets the high frequencies pass unaffected and operates only on the low-end sounds.

DJ

DAY 26: EQ TRICKS

- To learn the range of tricks that can be performed using EQ.

- To execute a few of these tricks smoothly.

THEORY

The extent to which you can perform EQ during a mix depends entirely on what sort of EQ your mixer has, so if possible you should keep this in mind when choosing your next mixer. Basically, the better the EQ, the better tricks you can perform with it.

THOUGHT FOR THE DAY

EQ is a strange beast that can be used to fix big problems as well as to enhance an already excellent mix.

The simplest EQ trick is cutting the bass. The gist of this trick is straightforward: to start with, EQ out the low end for the duration of a phrase (or for a couple of bars at the end of a phrase), then bring it back in at the beginning of the next phrase to add another big moment that otherwise wouldn't occur in the record. If your mixer has three EQ pots (treble, mid and bass), this is usually done with the bass EQ pot by turning it all the way down (anti-clockwise) at the desired moment and then turning it back to the zero position on the first beat of the next phrase. While this sounds easy, it takes practice to master the movements. It's vital that you turn the pot so quickly that it sounds almost like a switch has turned off the bass. And when you turn it back to zero again, remember not to go beyond the midway position or you'll find that your mix has too much boom, and might even blow the amp. Be careful and practise this with the volume down).

This trick can also be done using the HPF, and in much the same way. The only difference is that it's made easier by the fact that HPFs are usually smaller and more drastic and therefore easier to spin or pull down and up quickly. If your mixer has separate EQ controls for each channel, a whole further world of EQ tricks opens up. By manipulating the EQ of two records independently, the DJ is able to mix together records that would ordinarily be unmatchable.

The main advantage of separate-channel EQ is that you can run the bass of one record against the treble of another in order to create a new record in real time, in effect, with the bass of one playing under the vocals, high-frequency drums, strings and piano of the other. By the same token, with this technique you could mix together two records that seem to match except that they each have fat bass lines which are far too boomy to mix simultaneously.

As usual, start by beatmixing the two tunes. Then, just before making the switchover, turn down the bass in one of the records and mix the new one in. It's a good idea to practise with the two records at home to make sure that your EQ is powerful enough to achieve this radical goal.

Another handy trick for bass EQ is useful when drop-mixing or beatmixing two records that have big bass sounds or bass lines, which tend to weigh down the overall sound during a changeover. Just remember, as you pull down the EQ on one record or the other during the changeover, to pull it back up again as soon as possible in order to avoid any weak moments in your mix.

Careful use of bass EQ is also an excellent tool for cheating and giving the impression of tightly locked beats, even when your beatmixing is drifting a bit. Clearly, your aim should always be to mix as tightly as possible, but in a pinch a little downward tweak of bass EQ always makes things seem a little better than they actually are.

As a final advanced EQ trick, the high- and low-pass filters (if your mixer has both) can be used to simulate a sort of 'acid' sound on any record. Put a hand on each filter and begin by slowly turning the HPF – and if the LPF pot has an up as well as a down direction (some do, some don't), slowly turn up the LPF at the same time. When you've reached the limit, and the music sounds very trebly and thin, slowly reverse the process by turning the HPF back the other way. When the music has reached 'normal' again, immediately start turning the LPF. When you reach the limit this time, and the music sounds all bassy and muddy, slowly reverse the process again until you hit 'normal', then repeat the whole thing from the start. This creates that psychedelic sound usually associated with the Roland TR-303. Use a very repetitive section of a tune to get the best results.

EXERCISE

Have a go at performing the various tricks described above and try to invent your own personal variations on them.

Remember to listen to the speakers when performing these techniques because EQ tricks – if they can be heard at all – will always sound less pronounced and noticeable over headphones, as they don't convey the fuller sound of proper speakers.

On mixers that have controls allowing you to select EQ frequencies, the best bass

frequency for cutting the bass is usually around 80–180Hz.

DAY 27: LEVELS AND VOLUME THEORY

- To understand the fundamentals of how volume affects a mix.

- To learn how to use volume to create a smoother mix.

THEORY

Here's a rare moment in science when two plus two doesn't always equal four. When two records are playing at the same time, the overall volume will only be as loud as the louder of the records until they come within a certain level of each other. In other words,

THOUGHT FOR THE DAY

Louder ain't always better!

while one record is playing, you can begin to bring the volume of the second record up without affecting the overall volume in the speakers at all, until you get the volume of the second record within 3dB of the first one. (Usually, this means within a couple of notches on the mixer fader.) As soon as you reach those last crucial notches on the second fader, the overall volume in the speakers will go up (as you would expect, with two records playing instead of one), so you'll need to compensate by slightly bringing down the level of the first record. A clever balancing movement is now required while you bring up the second fader to its height and take the first fader down a bit more, then a bit more, until the first fader (which is now on its way down) hits that crucial point – a couple of notches lower down – where it stops having any effect on the overall volume. This is the point at which the second fader must be kept in order to keep the volume constant.

This is the goal, anyhow. You must keep the overall volume absolutely constant – or, if you're trying to do some flash trick with volume, at least under your control. If the overall volume is heard to fluctuate, the mix's smoothness and fluidity may be lost.

Of course, you're right to be thinking, 'Doesn't the crossfader do this for me?' Well, yes, it does, and most of the time it will and you won't think about this 'level theory' malarkey. But occasionally you'll want to manipulate it yourself, and this is when it's necessary for you to know about the two-plus-two-doesn't-equal-four business. The most common reason for mixing without the crossfader – ie with just the channel faders – is because the crossfader uses just one fader for both channels and therefore offers only half the fader length for each channel. Using the channel faders gives you more room for subtlety.

The other key idea here is that the loudest parts of a record aren't the things that your mind tends to focus on; the loudest bits are almost always the bass drum and the bass line (except when they aren't there, such as during a breakdown) and very rarely things like vocals. The bass drum and bass line are always in mono, so they will always make both left and right of the stereo sound move together. This is convenient because you can always use the level of the VU meters on your mixer to compare the levels of two tracks and thereby keep them identical.

EXERCISE

Try beatmixing two records using only the channel faders, aiming for as smooth a mix as you could achieve with the crossfader.

DJ

DAY 28

WEEK 4 TEST

Week 4 explored the fundamentals of EQ, tone and levels and how they can be exploited for effects and tricks. This test should highlight any problem areas.

1   What is the full range of the audio frequency spectrum?

2   What frequencies are the averages for low, mid and high EQ settings?

3   What are the two basic types of EQ?

4   What is a reference record?

5   What is an HPF?

WEEK 5

DAY 29: TRICKS – BACK-TO-BACK MIXING

TODAY'S GOALS

- To master the basics of back-to-back mixing.

- To attempt the more creative aspects of this trick.

THEORY

This is a simple trick to perform but one that is hard to perform well. The basic concept is that two records are played together half a beat apart (that is, back to back) and the DJ cuts in extra beats from the second record now and then to spice up the drum pattern in the first record.

THOUGHT FOR THE DAY

Every beat of music can be divided into two smaller halves, which themselves can be divided again until the divisions are too small and fast to hear.

Start by cueing up two copies of the same record – one on each deck – and listen to one of them in order to choose a section of constantly banging drums to practise with and a drop-in point that you can use as the main phrase when performing the trick. Now match the tempos of the two decks and cue up the second record just before your selected drop-in point. When the first record reaches the drop-in point, start up the second record to beatmix it in as usual. When you've got both records perfectly beat matched (in the headphones only, remember, because the crowd is hearing only the first record at this point), nudge the second record just a bit on the side to slow it down – and continue to slow it, bit by bit, until it's exactly half a beat behind the first record.

DJ

Remember the music lesson that we began with so many days ago, where we identified four beats in the bar which are usually marked with the boom-boom-boom-boom of four bass drums? Well, in fact the beats of music don't stop there; between each bass drum there is a half beat (usually marked by the 'peasoup' sound of an open hi-hat cymbal), and between the half beats there are quarter beats (often marked by shakers or maracas or some such smallish sound). For now, though, we'll stick with the half beats for these purposes.

DIVIDING THE BEAT

Beats	1				2				3				4		
Half beats	1		2		2		2		3		2		4		2
Quarter beats	1	2	3	4	2	2	3	4	3	2	3	4	4	2	3	4

The idea is that the two records should run together but half a beat apart so that each resultant bar of music contains, in effect, eight bass drums – that is, the four on the first record plus the four on the second running in between them.

Now comes the trick. With the two records running half a beat apart – and only the first record in the mix, because the crossfader is on the left – cut in extra bass drums from the second record by flicking the crossfader over to the other side and then, very quickly, all the way back on the half beat. This should give a single bass-drum hit in the mix between two normal bass drums from Record 1.

It's important that you do this smoothly and quickly, and even more important that you never lose the force of the pulse of the beats from Record 1. Always remember that the crowd is dancing to Record 1, and they'll lose it if you do much of this beat-confusing trickery. A little bit of this spice goes a long way.

When you've become adept at cutting in a single beat about once every other bar or so, try adding two or three extra beats at a time, always being careful not to lose the main pulse of Record 1.

Start practising this trick using a simple house record of about 120bpm. The four-on-the-floor bass drums are much easier to manipulate.

DAY 30: PHASE TRICKS

TODAY'S GOALS

- To understand the meaning of the term *phasing*.

- To learn how to create a phase effect.

THEORY

Phasing is an acoustic phenomenon that results from two identical sounds occurring almost – but not quite exactly – simultaneously. Because it is physically impossible for a human to spin two records at exactly and precisely the same time, the tiny inaccuracy that this produces – required to make the phasing effect – will always be present, even if you try to spin the records as perfectly synchronised as you can. In other words, aim for perfection and the trick will work anyway.

QUOTE FOR THE DAY

For phasing tricks, passages with lots of top-end percussion are often good because metalwork phases particularly well. – *DJ Phil Benedictus*

PHASING

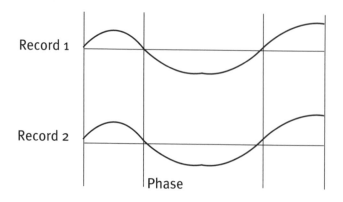

This trick requires two copies of the same record, just as before, playing together on the two decks. Start by tempo-matching the two records and, when the tempos are matched, cue them from the beginning of the tune and try to make them run as perfectly together as possible, as if one were 'hiding' exactly behind the other. When they're playing together, near as dammit, pull the crossfader to the middle in order to bring both records into the mix in equal volume. (Keep the overall volume down for this, as the combined sound of the two records might be quite loud.)

Now brush the side of Record 2 lightly to slow it down by just the tiniest amount. As you do this, you should hear a kind of psychedelic, metallic whooshing sound over the tunes themselves. After having slowed down Record 2, you'll need to do the same to Record 1 in order to slow it down and allow Record 2 to catch up. As you slow down each record in turn slightly, the effect increases and decreases with the changes in speed.

EXERCISE

Try the trick as described and see how far you can pull one record out of sync before the effect is lost (and then you'll need to cue them up and start again).

THOUGHT FOR THE DAY

Phasing is a great trick which has a hugely noticeable effect on your mix, but it can easily become obnoxious if overused, and it might even give some listeners headaches.

DAY 31: LINE/PHONO AND LEVEL TRICKS

TODAY'S GOALS

- To understand the potential of the Line/Phono switch.

- To understand the potential for tricks performed with only volume.

THEORY

Firstly, think back to the lessons from the first week and remember what the Line/Phono switch is. Each channel on the mixer has a Line/Phono switch on it which is meant to decide what that channel will listen

THOUGHT FOR THE DAY

The simplest things are usually the best.

to: either the turntable plugged into the Phono input on the back of that channel or to whatever may be plugged into the Line input on the back of that same channel. Since 99 per cent of all DJs will plug only a deck into the phono input on the back of a channel, and nothing at all into the line input of that channel, the Line/Phono switch will actually be switching between listening to the deck and listening to nothing (ie silence). So in practice, the Line/Phono switch functions as a 'kill switch' that instantly cuts out the sound on that channel and instantly restores it – and this is the simple basis for these tricks. The hard part here is to practise until you're dextrous enough to flick the switch as quickly and musically as if you were creating music from scratch on a keyboard or a saxophone. It takes time, but probably less than you might think.

Using the Line/Phono switch, you can create new rhythms from existing records by cutting out the sound in time with the record itself. One particularly effective use for this is to cut in and out on *a cappella* records in order to create a gated effect (like a sort of strobe-light effect but in sound). Another is to cut in and out on a drum beat just around the bass drums so as to allow only the bass drums to be heard, so that you hear just a big bass drum beating on the fours, without the other in-between drum sounds being heard. There are a million variations on the basic Line/Phono trick; you only need think of creative ways to cut in and out of your own mix.

The same sorts of tricks can also be done with the channel faders. While it might be more difficult to achieve the same speed with these as you can with the switch, you might find that you gain better control – especially for isolating bass drums and tiny sounds. Also, even if you prefer the switch technique, it pays to master the fader version because, at some point in your career, in all likelihood you'll encounter a mixer in a club with switches so dirty that such quick manipulation serves only to create horrible crackling noises, in which case fader tricks are your only option.

EXERCISE

Try to isolate the bass drums on a slowish record and then try quicker and quicker tunes until you reach your tempo limit. Remember this number, then try to improve on it during future practice sessions to develop your switch and fader techniques.

THOUGHT FOR THE DAY

For fast line/phono tricks, try using your thumb as a spring, pushing the switch one way against the finger pressure, and your finger to tap out rhythms against the pressure of the thumb.

CRASH COURSE

DJ

DAY 32: FILL TRICKS

- To understand the idea of dropping in fills.

- To learn how to drop various bars between records.

THEORY

Fill tricks are just the dropping-in of bits from other records over the current record. You could choose virtually any section in which to perform this, but the easiest choice is a loud, long or otherwise cool drum fill.

THOUGHT FOR THE DAY

Every little bit of added excitement makes for a better overall set

Start with a record playing on Deck 1 and the record with the drum fill on Record 2 and beat match them as usual . Once the tempos are the same, cue up Record 2 to a cue point eight bars before the fill. When Record 1 nears a spot eight bars before the point at which you want the fill, start up Record 2 and pull it into sync quickly so that both records are ready for the switchover.

The trick involves the usual manoeuvre with the crossfader, dropping in the fill over Record 1 and then moving quickly back to Record 1 so that only the fill from Record 2 is heard and Record 1 is heard immediately before and immediately after the fill. The hardest part is to guess the exact moment to switch over to the fill, and there's no way to do this if you don't know the records well enough to be able to predict the right moment. So, this trick requires knowledge and practice at home.

EXERCISE

Try choosing several different combinations of records where one has a fill or a short section to drop in to the other. Practise switching back to Record 1 right on the top of the following phrase.

Remember that many fills are of such uneven lengths that you can't count bars or beats to know when to switch; you just get to know the records so well that you feel the right moment.

DJ

DAY 33: A CAPPELLA MIXING

TODAY'S GOALS

- To learn what *a cappella* mixing is.

- To attempt some basic form of this trick.

THEORY

You will, of course, be familiar with 12" vinyl singles
featuring several mixes of the same tune. Usually there
is the radio mix and the extended mix, maybe a couple
of dub mixes and, less frequently, an *a cappella* mix
comprising the vocal track and nothing else.
Conversely, there will also frequently be an
instrumental version of the tune somewhere at the end of side B.

THOUGHT FOR THE DAY

**Many classic dance records were first conceived
through the happy accident of spinning vocal
records over completely different backing tracks.**

A cappella mixing is simply the art of beatmixing an *a cappella* mix over an
instrumental mix – although it must be said that this is not an easy thing to do; even
if you're able to start the beatmix well, it's twice as hard to keep it running.

You'll need to think long and hard and search far and wide to find two records that
are suitable for this trick and that truly work well together. The tunes need to be
close enough in tempo that the pitchshifting doesn't turn the singer into either
Mickey Mouse or Darth Vader. They also need to be in some sort of harmonious
relationship so that the combination doesn't actually hurt the ear.

Choose any two tracks that seem to be at roughly the same tempo (and hopefully close to the same key as well) and start by playing the backing track's tune. Do as well as you can to beat match the vocal track, although this type of beatmixing is difficult because there are no drums or obvious beats on the vocal track to use as reference; you'll need to listen to the vocal track quite closely to hear the rhythm and follow it without getting lost. Even more problematic is the fact that the vocal track will probably go out of sync before you notice any obvious problem. The good news, however, is that, since there aren't any drums telling you where the beat is, the audience will also be slow to notice any problems, so you'll have a lot more room for error.

The whole exercise is very much an intuitive one and improves over time. Don't be put off, though, even if, after you've mastered one combination, a different set of vocal and drum tracks takes you back to square 1. Every record is a new experience.

EXERCISE

Find two records that are suitable – even if only remotely – and try out this technique. When making speed adjustments on the a cappella record, try to use only the varispeed, as hand nudges tend to make the vocal sound wobbly, and try to make the necessary adjustments only in between the singing – ie while the singer takes a breath or rests – so that your speed changes aren't heard in the speakers.

DAY 34: THREE-DECK MIXING

TODAY'S GOALS

- To contemplate the awesomeness of three-deck mixing.

- To try it – or consider trying it – in practice.

THEORY

Three-deck mixing is clearly at least one-third more difficult than all other DJ skills. It requires that your beatmixing skills are very advanced, that you're well versed in the details of the records in your collection

THOUGHT FOR THE DAY

Three-deck mixing is the Formula 1 of DJing.

and that you must be quite quick at changing records. If you're feeling a bit cocky with your basic skills and you fancy a go, however, the possibilities are endless. Mostly, the three-deck world involves combinations of tricks that we've already learned, although there are also plenty of further possibilities that are entirely unique to mixing with a third deck.

The classic use of the third deck is to simply keep a sound-effects record on it at all times and to spin some weird or funny sounds over the top of your normal two-deck mix. Some DJs will use an actual sci-fi or sound-effect record with sounds like wind blowing or alien noises and just drop in a little weird ambience from time to time to keep things interesting (or to cover a poorly executed mix). Others will use themes of TV shows or speech to keep it all on the lighter side.

The real Three-Deck Heavies, however, will show off their skills by combining the most difficult of the basic skills in impressive ways. A favourite is to mix an *a cappella* track over top of two copies of the same backing track in order to drop in simultaneously bits of back-to-back mixing under the *a cappella* in progress. Obviously, this no easy trick, as it requires constant monitoring of the beat match of the *a cappella* mix and using the odd spare moment to hit the crossfader for a back-to-back drop-in – all the while being sure that the two backing tracks are still beat matched. Try this at home before the gig, please!

Other popular combinations include phasing, back-to-back mixing and keeping a source record for fills on Deck 3 which can be dropped in for the occasional fill.

EXERCISE

If you haven't got a third deck, try to arrange a day when you can borrow one from a mate for a few hours to try out some of the ideas mentioned above.

Don't forget that your priority is to keep the underlying mix going well. When things get sticky in a three-deck situation, drop the third deck and quickly return to the task of keeping the groove going from the main two decks.

DJ

DAY 35

Week 5 looked at ways in which you can make your mixing more interesting,

introducing you to some of the tricks and techniques used by top DJs.

EXERCISE

1   What is back-to-back mixing?

2   What is phasing?

3   For what purpose is the Line/Phono switch meant to be used?

4   What is a classic use for a third deck?

WEEK 6

DAY 36: FX AND DELAY

- To understand what delay is.

- To understand how delay is used in music.

THEORY

The word *delay* is closely connected to the word *echo*: they both involve producing a sound and waiting for it to bounce off the other side of Cheddar Gorge and come back to you. An echo, however, refers only to that

THOUGHT FOR THE DAY

Delay is the starting point for all sound effects.

specific incidence when you say something and can hear it distinctly a couple of seconds later. This happens because the valley or gorge that you're in is huge and your voice has to travel a long way before it's reflection comes back to you. Sound, unlike light, travels pretty slowly (in fact, some airplanes go faster), so it takes more than a second for your voice to get from your mouth to the other side of the canyon, bounce off the wall and travel back to you. And because it takes a full second to travel that distance, it arrives well after you've stopped speaking, so you can hear it clearly and distinctly.

THOUGHT FOR THE DAY

Search your records for examples of clearly distinct echoes and less distinct delay effects.

If you're in a small room – your bedroom, say – the same thing happens as in the
canyon, only more quickly. This time the sound travels only about eight feet – from
your mouth to the opposite wall and back again to your ear – and it makes it there and
back in about a tenth of a second or less. In this scenario, the echo returns to your ear
so soon after you've finished speaking that it's drowned out by your original speaking
voice, so you can't hear it. When it's this fast, it's indistinct and unnoticed and we
don't call it an echo; instead it's a delayed signal or, commonly, a *delay*.

Since we're all accustomed to hearing music played in rooms and halls and clubs and
stadiums, the distances involved are relatively small and the time it takes for the
music to bounce off the walls and return to us is very short. This is why the majority of
music effects tend to use tiny measurements of time – most commonly less than one
second – and usually measured in milliseconds (thousandths of a second).

Now, it's true that one-thousandth of a second (or one millisecond, or 1ms) is a very
short time indeed – probably quicker than the time it takes you to say the word *bit* –
but 500 milliseconds (or 500ms, and better known as half a second) is not so short;
it probably takes you less than 500ms to say the word *potato*.

The reason why all this is important is because, although delays or echoes of one or
two seconds don't really add anything except a gimmick during a nature hike, short
delays of under one second have a huge effect on the original sound. A delay on a
voice of about 500ms will make the singer sound as though he is singing at Wembley
Stadium, while a delay of 5ms will make him sound as though he's a Martian.

In music, delay is added to a sound by using a DDL (digital delay) effects box, which is a device added to the signal chain near the mixer stage and which acts as a sort of short-term storage shed. The DDL receives the sound at its input and stores the sound for a very short time (usually one second or less) before spitting it out the other end at the precisely required moment – such as, say, 35ms later. The delayed sound is then combined with the original dry (ie uneffected) sound to make a new sound which is the product of that mixture. The new sound depends entirely on the length of the added delay. This product of the DDL is the basis for all the normal weird and wonderful sounds present in modern recorded music, especially dance music.

EXERCISE

Using a clock with an easy-to-read second hand, study how long a second is by seeing how many words you can fit into one. Try it again for half a second, quarter of a second and an eighth of a second. As a DJ, it's useful to know how long one second really is.

DAY 37: DELAY EFFECTS

- To understand the effects that result from certain delay times.

- To recognise a few common delay effects by formal names and trade names.

THEORY

Shorter delay times does not equate to less noticeable effects. The shortest possible delay times (of even less than one millisecond) will change the sound of a record fundamentally, while some longer times (such as around 500ms) will muddy the sound of a record but won't make it unrecognisable.

THOUGHT FOR THE DAY

Pop music depends heavily on all the various delay effects.

Certain delay times create specific effects, and this is most clearly demonstrated when using the sound we all know best: the human voice. When a human voice is given a delay time of over one second, as we saw before, this gives the effect of an echo, as if the speaker/singer were in the mountains. When the time is shortened to between one-quarter and three-quarters of a second, the effect is as if he were performing in a stadium. When the time is less than about 100ms, the delayed sound occurs so quickly after the dry sound that the ear cannot distinguish the two and the result is one of the singer's own voice taking on a changed quality. By varying the delay time a few milliseconds longer and shorter than the target time (known as *modulation* of the delay time), well-known special effects can be created.

CRASH COURSE DJ

DELAY TIMES AND EFFECTS

Over 250ms: distinct echo

90ms–250ms: slapback – a quick repeat of the sound (used by John Lennon and most country-and-western singers)

50ms–80ms: double effect – as if two singers were trying to sing as one

30ms–50ms: chorus effect – giving a thicker quality to the voice, with fuller tone

10ms–30ms: flange effect – giving it a slightly 'underwater' quality – more body and a thicker tone

0.01ms–10ms: phasing effect – a metallic whooshing which alternates between very muffled and very trebly

For most purposes, you don't need to know the details of the theory behind time delays in sound, because the manufacturers have handily made boxes that enable you simply to dial up the desired effect, and they use the slang terms like chorus, flange, phase and so on.

However, it's always possible to do further editing of the factory-set pre-programmed effects on most effects units, but even so it's very difficult to edit them properly if you have no idea what a delay effect is. And now you do. Well done!

EXERCISE

Search your record collection for examples of the above delay effects and try to identify them as such, thinking about the way in which each is created.

THOUGHT FOR THE DAY

When editing delay effects in factory-set programs, don't change the delay times, because these are what's making the effect in the first place. Instead, try adjusting the modulation rate and listen to the subtle – but effective – results.

CRASH COURSE

DJ

DAY 38: WHAT IS REVERB?

- To understand what reverb is.

- To understand how it's used in music.

THEORY

It's easy to know when someone has telephoned you from the bathroom. We all recognise the telltale sound of 'man in bathroom': his voice has a tin-can quality and each word rings for a short moment after he's spoken. Equally, we all recognise the sound of God's voice in Hollywood movies: he's clearly in a very large room and each word sprays out after it's spoken, rather like water spraying up and out from a waterfall.

THOUGHT FOR THE DAY

Every sound you've ever heard – both recorded and live – has some kind of reverb on it.

Both of these sounds are examples of reverb. Just as with delay and echo, every sound that's ever created will fly out in all directions, bounce off every available surface and then hit our ears just as many times. When a teacher speaks to his class, his voice travels first of all directly from his mouth to his students' ears – but it also travels in the other direction and hits the wall, bounces off and then goes into their ears. And of course it also travels in all the other directions, bouncing off all the other walls, the ceiling and floor, and travelling (probably with a couple of further bounces) to their ears again. All in all, the teacher's voice is probably hitting the students' ears many thousands of times before dying away – but, because the

room is small, this all happens in less than a few milliseconds and the students
can't distinguish the 'dry' sound of the voice from all the subsequent reflections, so
they don't perceive it as reverb.

Of course, if the speaker is onstage in Carnegie Hall, the distances are much greater
and the walls are not so square and parallel, so it may take a couple of seconds or
even longer (up to about five seconds, probably) for all the reflected sounds to
arrive at the listener's ear. This time, the listener perceives the reverb; he thinks to
himself, 'This is a large room. I must be in Carnegie Hall!'

The only places on Earth where a sound is almost entirely without any reverb at all
are open fields; here, the sound has nothing (except the ground) to bounce off, and
so there are no reflections. This is why it's always easy to tell when a speaker is
talking outside: his voice has that 'outside' quality to it, with no reverb. If a record
was to feature a lead singer's performance without any reverb, it would sound
strange and very exposed, so very few singers are willing to be represented in this
way (although Suzanne Vega was, famously, one of them).

Reverb is perhaps slightly less relevant to DJs because all records will already have
some reverb on them, and so they need not bother doing anything more. However, if
you find yourself armed with a multi-FX box equipped with reverb programs, you
might find that the effect has its uses. If you add further reverb to a record, the
result can be interesting and, possibly, useful to an arty DJ.

EXERCISE

Search your collection for vocal records that use

noticeable reverb effects and try to find both very short

and very long reverb examples.

THOUGHT FOR THE DAY

Think about the reverb aspects of records that mix

well together – are they similar or different? Is this

one of the reasons why they seem to work well

together?

DAY 39: REVERB EFFECTS

TODAY'S GOALS

- To understand the effects that result from certain reverb times.

- To learn about a few common reverbs by formal names and trade names.

THEORY

This lesson overlaps somewhat with the field of music production, so if or when you finally begin your first attempt at making a record – or even if you've already done so – remember to check this again for helpful guidance.

THOUGHT FOR THE DAY

Adding more reverb from the DJ's own effects box can add drama to a mix.

Reverb is generally produced by multi-FX boxes, which also offer most of the other common effects used in music production – ie delay effects, EQ, compression, gating and so on. The usual version of these boxes has two inputs and two outputs, with each pair handling stereo left and right, so really its just one input and one output. A sound source, such a vocal track, is fed into the input and the sound of the reverb comes out of the output. The reverb must be combined with the dry sound (usually a roughly equal mix) in order to create properly the effect of a singer singing in Carnegie Hall (or wherever, depending on the chosen reverb setting).

The trick is that a single sound can be fed into the box or the entire mix can be fed into it. The difference is huge: either the singer is placed in a good-sounding room, with glistening tones spraying after each note, or the entire record is in that room.

Generally, applying reverb to an entire mix is not done because it tends to make things sound so muddy and washy – although this might be exactly the thing to do during your mix at the gig to achieve a wild moment and bring down the house.

Reverbs are meant to simulate all the various spaces in the world. The most important factor determining the overall sound is the length of the reverb, which is called *decay time*. This is the time it takes for the 'spray' of the reverb to die out. As a rule, short decay times, which don't cloud up the mix, are about 1–1.5 seconds long, and the longest times, which can sound like the mix is falling off a cliff into the Grand Canyon, are about 4–6 seconds.

REVERB TIMES AND EFFECTS

0.1–0.5 seconds: tiny broom closet; very dampened sound

0.5–1.0 second: small bedroom; ambient but still tight sound

1.0–1.5 seconds: small wood-floored or empty room; adds body or life to any sound

1.5–2.5 seconds: large empty room; creates grandeur and plenty of ambience

2.5–4.0 seconds: concert hall; gives a soaring feel and maybe even goosebumps

4.0–6.5 seconds: cavernous, concrete, indoor arena; the sound rings on and on...

THOUGHT FOR THE DAY

For a big, crowd-pleasing moment, try putting the entire mix into a reverb box for just one beat and then quickly pulling it out again and letting that one beat of music ring in the reverb over the ongoing dry mix.

EXERCISE

If you haven't got a reverb unit, either in the mixer or a free-standing model, try to borrow one from a friend for a day. Feed an *a cappella* record into it and start with a pre-set program with a decay time of about 1.5 seconds and work up and then down from there to hear what the different reverbs sound like. Notice which decay time is programmed into which program name (ie 'large room' is probably about two seconds).

DJ

DAY 40: STROBE (TEMPO) EFFECTS

TODAY'S GOALS

- To understand what the strobe tricks are.

- To learn how to perform a strobe trick.

THEORY

This technique consists of slowing down the tempo by using the hand to pause the record on every beat count, delaying one record against the other and fading back and forth between the two records. The two records can be the same or two completely different beats. The DJ begins by slowing the first record, then takes the second and delays it by a given number of beat counts and alternately pauses and fades between the two decks.

EXERCISE

Try to perform the trick as described above.

THOUGHT FOR THE DAY

It's OK to show off, but make sure you've got the trick perfected before going for it in public!

DAY 41: BREAKDOWNS AND SPINBACKS

TODAY'S GOALS

- To be able to perform a breakdown.

- To be able to perform a spinback.

THEORY

The breakdown is similar to the strobe trick, although it's easier because there's only one thing to think about. The trick is a manual slowdown of the beat by using your hand to rhythmically stop the record on each beat. It takes some practice to get good at stopping the record and letting it go again quickly, and to do it evenly so that it sounds like the tempo is gradually slowing down.

THOUGHT FOR THE DAY

For extra shock value, turn the power off while the record is playing and let it slow down and stop. Then, slowly at first, spin it back – gradually getting faster – until you suddenly cut the channel fader, put the needle back to the beginning of the tune and jam it back into the mix.

The spinback is a classic trick that goes with the expression 'rewind!' and it is an excellent vehicle for showing off, if that's what you want to do. On the last beat of the last bar of the phrase, when you're about to mix out of that record, spin the record back very suddenly and sharply on the slipmat. Then crossfade away from that record right on the first beat of the next bar, which should be the beginning of a new phrase on the second record, as usual. (Note that records which are even slightly warped will not spin back properly.)

DJ

Achieving successful breakdowns and spinbacks requires practice.
Gently does it!

DAY 42

WEEK 6 TEST

Week 6 introduced you to reverb and delay and showed you to how to use them in

your own mixing. Remember: only practice makes perfect!

1 What is a DDL?

2 What is the difference between a delay and an echo?

3 How short must a delay be to not be heard as distinct from the original sound?

4 What is reverb?

5 What is a strobe effect?

WEEK 7

DAY 43: SCRATCHING

TODAY'S GOALS

• To understand what scratching is.

• To understand where scratching came from and why it evolved as it did.

THEORY

Scratch DJing – *turntablism* – is the skill of manipulating a sound by hand, using a record as a sound source and a crossfader to edit it, usually in time to other music (ie using the deck as a musical instrument in its own right). It's usually executed with just one sound from a record which is repeated by passing that small section of vinyl under the needle and physically pulling it back to the original position to start again.

QUOTE FOR THE DAY

The art of scratching is not what DJs do to their heads while deciding which tune to play next. – *DJ David Sloly*

The whole process is spontaneous and fully live, so success depends entirely on the dexterity and talent of the DJ on the night. As with traditional musical performance, everything is at stake for the DJ and lost nerves can wreck a show.

THOUGHT FOR THE DAY

Always carry an extra slipmat or two because a wet slipmat (damp from sweat dripping on it in a hot club or a spilled beer or whatever) won't slip and you'll need a quick change.

As legend has it, scratching started as an accident by the then well-known New York DJ Grand Wizard Theodore in his Bronx bedroom in 1975. The story is that he was playing around on his turntable when his mother came in and, instead of hitting the start/stop button, he stopped it with his hand. Apparently, he just didn't want to hear what she had to say, so he started to rub the record back and forth, thus creating a scratching sound that drowned out whatever she was trying to say. Presumably it wasn't long before he realised that this could be done to great effect at a gig – and the rest, as the saying goes, is DJ history.

The best thing about scratching is that you don't need any special gear to do it – the normal basic DJ setup is the complete package – and, actually, you need only one deck. The slipmat is the magic secret to scratching (it would be otherwise impossible to manipulate the record under the needle), so make sure yours is properly slippy.

The hardest aspect of learning to scratch is simply keeping the needle in the groove. Make sure your tone arm is heavy enough, or at least slightly heavier than normal, and ensure that the table or surface you're working on isn't wobbly. The mixer is also likely to take some punishment, so make sure it's strong and in a healthy condition, and that it doesn't rock the decks when you use extra elbow grease.

When you're actually scratching a record, you're concerned with only one small section of grooves at a time and focusing on a specific sound, sometimes called a *sample*. When you pull the sound under the needle, the faster you pull, the higher the pitch of the sound, and the slower you pull, the lower the pitch.

Remember that, if you change the speed during the course of a single scratch, you

can make the sound change pitch as it plays (although this is difficult to pull off

unless the sound is a rather long one, such as a held vocal note, such as 'aaaahhhh').

EXERCISE

Attempt your first scratch. Choose a short vocal note from an *a cappella* mix and

start by slowly pulling the sample back and forth under the needle.

DAY 44: BASIC SCRATCHING – BABY, FORWARD

TODAY'S GOALS

- To perform a Baby scratch.

- To perform a Forward scratch.

THEORY

The Baby is the basic scratch on which all other scratches are based. Basically, it involves pulling a single, simple sound back and forth under the stylus in time to the music on the other deck. Start by playing a record on the second deck and cueing up your scratch sound on the first. Run the second tune and try doing just one scratch (one pull on the cued-up sound) on the first beat of the bar. Keep the moves short and clipped so that they sound like another drum playing along on the first beats of the running tune. Step up to a scratch on every other beat and then every beat.

Virtually any sound on a record can work for this basic scratch – drums, percussion, keyboard hits, big chords, vocal bits, you name it. And remember to keep your hand well clear of the tone arm while scratching to ensure that the needle doesn't jump.

The Forward scratch adds in some movement of the crossfader, so now you'll need both hands. The crossfader is used in this scratch to chop and stop the sound of the scratch being heard in the speakers (although, of course, you'll always hear all of your moves over the headphones). The trick is to get rid of any unwanted sounds by throwing the crossfader at the right times.

Since the tune on the second deck is always running and being heard (and providing the overall groove and beat to which you are scratching), the crossfader will at least be in the halfway position so that both decks are in the mix. With the Forward scratch, start with the crossfader all the way over toward the second deck and bring it to the middle only for the moments that you want the scratch sounds to be heard. The classic move is to pull the fader over to allow the sound of the scratch going forward but not the sound of it going in reverse, hence its name.

EXERCISE

Start practising the Baby scratch with a slow-tempo tune to make it easier to perform. Gradually speed up until you feel comfortable doing quite quick pulls and varying the speed of the scratches. For the Forward, use a kick-drum sound and pull over the crossfader with your other hand to allow the forward-running drum to be heard. Then quickly pull back the crossfader and pull back the sound (while it's not in the mix) and repeat the sound on top of the next bar. Keep practising this slow version until you're comfortable enough to break free of the pattern and play what you feel. The corollary of the Forward is the Backward scratch, which is the same thing, only in reverse. The basic steps are, for the Forward: crossfader open, forward scratch, crossfader closed, return record to original cue position, repeat. For the Backward scratch: crossfader closed, forward scratch, crossfader open, backward scratch, repeat.

THOUGHT FOR THE DAY

If you haven't got a workable slipmat, use a piece of a plastic bag by cutting a small hole in the middle and draping it over the platter.

DAY 45: SCRIBBLE AND CHOP

TODAY'S GOALS

- To perform the Scribble.

- To perform the Chop.

THEORY

The Scribble is just a twisted version of the Baby in which the sample

sounds...well, scribbled. Start by doing a basic Baby scratch, with the sound

occurring regularly (as before: silence – sample – silence). The trick here is to

shake your forearm (the one doing the scratching) quickly but not wildly, with

little actual movement back and forth. You can use the crossfader if you can think

of something clever or cool to do with it, but the essence of this scratch is to make

your arm (and the sample) freak out.

THOUGHT FOR THE DAY

It may help to move your body to the rhythm of
the running tune on Deck 2 in order to be sure that
your scratches are falling into the rhythms of the
main beat.

The Chop involves some pretty serious crossfader technique in addition to the Forward scratch moves. The goal here is to let only part of the Forward scratch be heard by 'chopping out' some of the sound with the crossfader. If the chosen sample to be scratched was, say, a long word from a vocal track, the Chop would allow only the first syllable of the word to be heard so as to tease the audience for a few seconds before letting the rest of the word play.

 DJ

This requires fast crossfader movement, so start by practising the crossfader moves

to improve your skill and speed. Use just one finger and thumb to grasp the

crossfader and practise flicking it in time to the music so that you can make several

groovy moves in a short time. Make sure you can perform the crossfader moves and

know where it is at all times, because – and this is important with all scratching –

you need to keep your eyes on the stylus at all times so that you know where to

return the needle to when re-cueing after a scratch. Furthermore, you won't have

adequate brainspace to think about the crossfader as well, as you'll have to be

thinking about the timing, the beat and the balance of the records in the mix.

EXERCISE

First, try the Scribble with the tone arm off the record to get comfortable with the

feel of shaking your arm while holding the record in the right place, then try it

without the safety net. For the Chop, there's no other way than to start slow and

work gradually faster. Also, try more complicated and shorter sounds to chop up.

DAY 46: TRANSFORMER AND CRAB

TODAY'S GOALS

• To perform the Transformer.

• To perform the Crab.

THEORY

The Transformer scratch builds on the Chop by creating a series of edits, or *chops*, on a single sound. This is quite difficult to get the hang of at first, so start with a very long vocal sample to practise on. As you slowly push the sample under the record, throw the crossfader back and forth repeatedly, very quickly and regularly, so that the sound is broken into as many equally sized pieces as possible. This effect is similar to the gated effect heard on many records from the '90s and is analogous to a strobe-light effect, but on a single sample. The effect may be even more pronounced if you can make it groove to the beat by throwing the crossfader back and forth on the beat, the half beat or, ideally, the quarter beat.

The Crab scratch utilises very, very fast repetitions within a Transformer-like scratch, and again takes a while to master. The essence of this trick is a hand manoeuvre like a finger-click that enables you to move the crossfader more quickly than you could do with just a normal finger-and-thumb flicking motion. The scratching part is easy – you just pull a long sample under the needle – but the crossfader move must be done in a way that initially seems bizarre.

To learn this elaborate manoeuvre, start by placing your thumb and fifth finger on the crossfader and then 'finger-click' so that the ring finger ends up in place of the fifth finger. Repeat the process but this time click to your third finger and then, finally, again so that you end up with your index finger on the crossfader. The idea is that the clicking of the fingers puts the crossfader in the 'off' position for just an instant for each finger, and so four different chops of the sound are heard. So, in the final version, snap all four fingers past the crossfader, and with many hours of practice the sound should 'crab'. Clearly, most people need a considerable amount of practice with one finger at a time before any amount of proficiency is attained. Good luck!

THOUGHT FOR THE DAY

Scratching is a physical performance, so make sure that your body posture and physical position in the booth are conducive to free movement.

EXERCISE

Try the scratches as described, but remember to take regular breaks as the Crab scratch can cause cramps and aches in your fingers.

DAY 47: RUB/STAB, FLARE AND ORBIT

TODAY'S GOALS

- To perform a Rub and a Stab.

- To perform the Flare.

- To perform the Orbit.

THEORY

The Rub and the Stab are much easier than the other scratches, so they give you a chance to think again about the basic skills in all the scratches. The Rub is, in fact, just a Baby scratch during which you slow down the record. When the speed decreases, the pitch falls and you get a sort of deceleration effect and that drags the sound through the mix. The motion needed for this is rather like rubbing the vinyl.

THOUGHT FOR THE DAY

While learning new scratches, keep practising the basic moves onto which to build the new skills.

The Stab is just the same but in reverse: push forward quite sharply as the sound begins playing to create a high-pitched shriek similar to the keyboard 'stabs' on many records. With both the Rub and the Stab, different sounds are produced when you go backwards.

The Flare scratch again utilises rapid crossfader moves. Start with the crossfader open on the scratch side and push the sound under the needle but cut the sound off by throwing over the crossfader and then immediately throw it back on again.

Pull the record back through again and repeat the crossfader off-and-on movements at the same time.

The speed of the crossfader moves must be lightning fast, so start as usual with a long sample for easy practice. The secret is to pinch the crossfader rather that flick it so that you can quickly turn it on and off in one movement. Use the thumb to switch it off and the finger to turn it back on.

The Orbit is performed by using an additional finger-click in the Flare scratch. Hover the crossfader right on the cut point and use the finger-click method to turn it off and then on again – only this time use two fingers in order to get the double-click result. Do the double-click for both directions of the scratch for the full Orbit scratch.

EXERCISE

Try the scratches as described above.

DJ

DAY 48: HYDROPLANE AND BEAT JUGGLING

TODAY'S GOALS

- To perform scratches using 'tones'.

- To perform the Hydroplane.

- To attempt beat-juggling.

THEORY

The 'tones' trick is a fantastic one for both the DJ and the audience. If you get it right, you can do it for quite a long time without either side getting bored. The huge problem with this trick, however, is that you need a specialised record to perform it with: one that has tones on it – either a test tone from a 'technical alignment for machines' record or, perhaps, a specially cut white-label disc (sometimes available from the best record shops). You'll just have to ask around.

THOUGHT FOR THE DAY

If you can't find a shop with a tones record, as a last resort call a mastering studio and get a quote for pressing a one-off white label of a tones disc (using a tone generated by an oscillator), which can usually be had reasonably cheaply.

Once you find such a beast, pop it on the deck and check out how obnoxious and seemingly useless it sounds – until you start scratching it. Start by using the Pitch control to vary the speed until the record hits a decent-sounding pitch against the record running on Deck 2. When the tone is matched musically to the other record, you can choose any bit of the tones record to perform any scratch and almost anything will sound brilliant, as if you were jamming a musical instrument live in your mix.

The Hydroplane is an eerie effect achieved by actually gliding your fingers along the vinyl grooves of the record in the opposite direction of the way it's spinning. Vary the pressure you use to create an underwater and gritty, muddyish sound.

Beat-juggling is not actually scratching, but DJs often perform the two together. The idea of beat-juggling (sometimes called *looping*) is to extend a section of a record by repeating it over and over again. For starters, you need two copies of the same record.

Cue up the same chosen section on both decks and set one running. When the end of the section arrives, beatmix in the same section on the other deck. Cue up the same section again back on the first deck, and repeat until the cows come home. The trick, however, is to make it so smooth that no one in the audience twigs about the second record, and this requires ultra-smooth switchovers between records. Use your best beatmixing technique (already learned and mastered, of course) and never take you eyes off the bits of vinyl (to ensure that you can quickly and accurately cue and re-cue the two records). After a few loops, shorten the section to a bar and then to half a bar (if you're quick enough) to achieve a trance-like effect in the mix, with the same half-bar playing over and over. When you get really good at this, deploy a few scratches here and there, to tease the crowd into thinking that you're going to break out of the beatmix, and then bring the loop back in again.

EXERCISE

Try the scratches as described here – that is, if you can find a tones record and two copies of a suitable tune.

DAY 49

The advanced techniques you learned this week can be used to add interesting and

dramatic effects to your DJing.

1 What is scratching?

2 Who is thought to have invented scratching?

3 What is a Baby scratch?

4 What is Transforming?

WEEK 8

DAY 50: CD AND DIGITAL MIXING

TODAY'S GOALS

- To understand the basic concepts underpinning MP3 technology.

- To understand the basics of digital DJing.

THEORY

You would be forgiven for asking why anyone would want to DJ with MP3 or digital sources when clearly you cannot touch the record and you can't find half the classic dance tracks on these formats, and you would be wise to heed these real concerns. But fret not – the advantages just about balance out the problems.

THOUGHT FOR THE DAY

Using digital elements in your setup doesn't stop you from using all the traditional gear alongside, or even at the same time.

CD MIXING

While you can't spin a compact disc with the hands-on approach, you can, of course, do it in a different way. Many DJ-model CD players have both the standard automatic mode and a manual mode for cueing up. In the Auto mode, the tune stops just before the beginning of the track – which is useless for DJing, as it doesn't enable you to start the track quickly enough. Players with a Manual mode will have a *jog wheel* (a massive round controller) that enables you to move the cue point similar to the way you would with vinyl, in that you can choose an exact spot much closer to the beat. This means you can mix with ease, as you need only hit the play button at the usual time and work the crossfader as usual, so cueing is convenient and familiar.

The sounds of the record even sound the same while cueing; that unique *kuh* of the bass drum heard when cueing vinyl is reassuringly recognisable. Up to five cue points can also be stored, enabling you to return to a pre-selected spot easily and instantly. The problem, however, is that the points cannot be saved when changing to a different disc, so it's a very transient and fleeting advantage.

MP3 MIXING

OK, so the MP3 format is rather more off-putting because there's nothing to hold on to or even look at. But, again, fret not, the advantages are many. An MP3 is a computer data file holding one full song. The magic of MP3 that distinguishes it from other computer-based music is that it is a compressed format – meaning that an average tune – which would normally use a hefty amount of data, perhaps as much as 40MB of memory – uses typically ten times less (or, typically, about 4MB) in MP3 format. The upshot of this is that MP3 files can be stored and shared far more efficiently.

Cueing up MP3 tracks is itself a DJing revolution – you can store as many cue points as you like and keep them forever. This means that, as soon as you choose to play a particular tune, you already have the ability to jump immediately to any exact spot in the tune previously stored in rehearsal at home. This means, therefore, no more hunting for cue points in the dark, and no need to remember all those physical places on a record; just look at the screen to find what you need instantly. As for quality, it's almost a dead issue; no one seems even to notice any difference – and even if they do, they certainly aren't too bothered.

Numark CDMIX2 dual CD player/DJ mixer

Try to find both the vinyl and MP3 versions of the same tune and listen to them both,

one after the other, to compare sound quality, cueing ease and any other noticeable

practical differences.

DAY 51: PITCH-SHIFTING AND BEAT MATCHING

TODAY'S GOALS

- To beatmix a CD.

- To beatmix an MP3.

THEORY

Beatmixing with these formats is usually done in conjunction with turntables,
since all DJs – even those devoted to digital formats – still do the lion's share of
their mixing on vinyl. Therefore, the following examples deal with beatmixing
digital tunes to vinyl.

THOUGHT FOR THE DAY

**Beware of MP3 automatic tempo adjustment, as it
can often be slightly wrong, often by just enough
to throw out a beatmix if you don't switch over
within a couple of bars.**

CD BEATMIXING

Beatmixing a CD is almost exactly the same as
beatmixing with vinyl, except the actual cueing up is
somewhat different (as described in yesterday's
lesson). Start by cueing the CD to the chosen spot
and, as the vinyl is approaching the drop point, hit
the Play button. The beat matching is as with vinyl,
except that you can't use your finger to affect the
speed so it must all be done with the pitch-
adjustment slider. All the DJ models generally have
excellent sliders that mirror the vinyl versions and
don't take much getting used to.

DJ

MP3 BEATMIXING

Due to the convenience of pre-saved cue points (as described in yesterday's lesson), beatmixing is, in one sense, dead easy. In another sense, however, since there is no actual pitch-adjustment slider on a normal computer, it appears to be impossible! The quick solution is, of course, always to use the MP3 as the first track and only to beatmix to it, and never to try the opposite direction. Obviously, you'll need to mix over to the MP3 at some point, so it's probably better simply to dropmix into it and save the beatmixing for the way out.

In fact, though, pitch adjustment on MP3 format is quite possible, and it's actually done for you by the computer. Some MP3-mixing software products (such as Visiosonic) will calculate the correct speed for the new record by listening to the previous tune, judging its tempo and digitally adjusting the MP3 to match. It might not be as much fun, but it certainly helps at the end of a night in a club that allows the DJ free drinks.

EXERCISE

Try beatmixing a CD as described above.

DJ

DAY 53: FINAL SCRATCH

- To understand what Final Scratch is.

- To understand the basic functions and potential of digital scratching.

QUOTE FOR THE DAY

Final Scratch is a great tool to catalogue my music. It has a great search engine. I DJ with CDs, but if you have books and books of CDs, how do you find things? In Final Scratch, you put in what you feel – it has a comment in the search engine what you think about the track. It has an artist field, a title field, whatever. I go with emotions, so if I want to play something sexy and deep because there are a lot of cute women out there, you know what? I put in 'sexy and deep'. That's how I labelled the track. Sometimes I go to gigs and I have no idea what kind of club it is – could be house, could be techno. This gives me the choice without having to bring seven boxes of records. I have 1,200 songs on my laptop. – *Josh Wink*

DJ

Despite the numerous advantages of MP3 mixing, most DJs are instantly repulsed by the very suggestion of DJing with only a mouse in their hand. Not only is manipulation of 'virtual decks' onscreen with a mouse very limited, but it's also dead boring to watch and – worse still – to perform.

Final Scratch is an incredibly clever solution to these inherent problems. The product uses as an interface a traditional turntable with which the DJ manipulates the MP3 files in the computer. The turntable plays only one record, however, which only the computer listens to.

Instead of music in its grooves, the record has a constant stream of computer data called SMPTE time code, which is essentially just a digital clock pressed into the record grooves. When the needle passes over the record, it transmits the corresponding clock time to the computer – ie at the beginning of side A, the computer reads '0:00', and when the needle is two minutes in, it reads '2:00'. The best part is that, by comparing the data received with its own internal clock, the computer knows whether you're spinning the record fast or slow or forward or backward.

The computer runs software that assigns a timer to the MP3 song so that, if you drop the needle at any point on the vinyl, the computer immediately jumps to the corresponding point in the MP3. If you stop the vinyl with your hand and scratch it back, the computer stops the tune and plays that corresponding bit backwards sharply, just as if it was in the grooves (traditionally speaking).

All the components necessary for a Final Scratch setup

Of course, the DJ still must choose the song he requires onscreen and work the

program in order to send the tunes to the mixer, but at least the vinyl plays a central

role and the DJ is able to get hands-on in every normal way.

EXERCISE

Visit www.stanton-magnetics.com or www.switch52.com and read updated or

further material on Final Scratch to see if this is a route that suits your style.

DJ

DAY 54: PC CONNECTIONS AND SETUPS

- To find out the gear required for PC DJing.

- To understand the basics of PC DJing connections.

THEORY

There are many different software applications available for the PC, all of which provide the necessary bits for a PC-only setup (clearly not including amp, speakers and headphones). There are no names of specific software manufacturers mentioned here, rather just the important generic elements to keep in mind when you're choosing the products most suitable for you.

DJ software applications – even the free ones that can be downloaded from dozens of websites – are designed as self-contained packages. They usually feature an onscreen representation of two virtual decks and a virtual mixer. Using the mouse and the computer keyboard, the decks can be loaded, cued, spun and manipulated, and the mixer can be worked as you would expect from a video-game version of a DJ booth. You can listen to the sound via the computer's own speakers or your own add-on speakers plugged into the Sound Output hole at the back. But, of course, the sound quality is only slightly better than your average clock radio, and the full extent of the control knobs is a power switch and a volume knob.

Every PC has a built-in (or factory-installed) *soundcard*, which is just the IT word for the computer component that converts the digital numbers into actual sound. The built-in version is typically of quite poor quality but, more importantly, it offers only the tiny, mini-jack socket at the back for you to connect slightly better-quality (though still low-power) speakers.

It is entirely possible – and quite fun, for a while – simply to use the DJ software and mix your MP3s among themselves, leaving your proper DJ gear to rest quietly. Assuming that you prefer to use both the traditional and digital-format gear at the same time to raise your game to unprecedented heights, the options available to you are threefold.

OPTION 1: THE BARE MINIMUM

This option requires only the bog-standard soundcard (even the factory version will do). You'll need to separate somehow the two channels coming out of the Sound Output hole at the back of the computer. If you're lucky, there will be two holes already (labelled 'left' and 'right'); if not, visit a stereo shop and buy a splitter (or 'Y') cable that splits the single stereo signal via two mono sockets or plugs.

Connect the left side to your headphones (you might need further adaptors) and the right side to a channel of a DJ mixer (you might need another splitter to get the one wire into both the input sockets of the mixer). Then configure the onscreen virtual mixer so that the virtual headphone sound comes out of only the left side, while the master-mix output comes out of only the right side.

OPTION 2: A BETTER SOLUTION

This option requires a slightly more up-market soundcard providing two sets of stereo sound outputs, labelled 'Front' and 'Rear' (or, sometimes '1', '2', '3' and '4'). Use the Front outputs for your headphones and plug the Rear outputs into a channel of your mixer, then configure the virtual mixer so that the cue sound for the headphones goes to the front outputs and the master mix output goes to the rear outputs.

OPTION 3: THE BEST SOLUTION

This is the preferred option and, unsurprisingly, requires two separate sound cards in your PC. As you will have already guessed, you use one soundcard and its outputs for the headphones and the other card for the connection to your mixer.

Whatever method you use, the hardest part will be getting used to mixing with two separate mixers which are both active at the same time. You'll need to work both the virtual mixer and the real mixer constantly to ensure that the sound coming out of the PC is cued, beat matched, levelled and configured correctly while at the same time conducting your normal business on the DJ mixer. It might sound horrible, but in fact it doesn't take so long to find that you're actually comfortable with the arrangement and even prefer it to having just the normal one mixer and two decks.

THOUGHT FOR THE DAY

Splitter cables and adaptors should be very cheap items. If you suspect that you're being over-charged, check the Internet for average prices.

DJ

DAY 55: RIPPING, ENCODING AND ONLINE DATABASES

TODAY'S GOALS

- To understand the concepts and implications of ripping and encoding.

- To be aware of the potential of online databases and the advantages offered to DJs.

THEORY

Music stored on a computer in MP3 format can be mixed and manipulated easily, but it can't be shared very easily via cyberspace (except if sent by email, but most email accounts are too small or the connections too slow to make this viable). Furthermore, as MP3 files are mostly over 3MB in size, they don't fit on floppy disks.

THOUGHT FOR THE DAY

In cyberspace, no one can hear you rip...

The logical option, then, is to store the files on a CD or CD-ROM. (For these purposes, a 'CD' is an audio disc that can be played in a CD player and a 'CD-ROM' is a data-only CD that the user must put into a computer to extract the data. The data can then be played back as a sound file.) The act of burning a recordable CD is known as *ripping*, which is clearly derived from the expression 'ripping off'! Because of the apparent permanency of the CD format, it's generally thought that burning a CD from a piece of music is somehow a more aggressive act than just emailing a file or storing it on a disc. Of course, this is a silly notion, since whatever motive there may be, the result is the same regardless of the medium, but nevertheless the sentiment is strong. As a result of this kind of thinking, it seems that it might be safer not to discuss ripping with people employed in the record industry.

Encoding, meanwhile, refers to the act of burning an MP3 file onto a CD, but it generally means that you're talking about the quality level being used. We've already seen that the whole issue of quality is hardly relevant to DJs, since the reduced frequency range is still well within the smaller limits that club systems reproduce anyway, but it might someday be important to know that the minimum standard for decent quality is 192kbps (kilobits per second) as the sampling rate (ie the rate at which the computer analyses the music and then stores it). A higher rate is obviously better, though, and many people prefer 256kbps.

Once you become handy at acquiring and storing MP3 files, you'll soon find that, as with vinyl, you can't have too many. As a distinct advantage over vinyl, though, a large MP3 collection is far easier to organise and handle because, aside from it weighing a million times less, the MP3 collection can be searched with the touch of a button. It is important to develop a system for naming the files that is consistent and easy to use – but then, labelling methods and organisation systems are as varied and unique as, say, personal grooming habits. Needless to say, constantly backing up your collection is a must so that you don't lose anything if your computer crashes.

The main great advantage of digital music collecting, however, is that the record shop is always open online – not to mention that the prices are unbeatable (often as not, the tunes are free). Plus, online databases for music – from which tunes can be downloaded – are too numerous to single any one out, but if you've never done it before, try searching for artist names, song names or genre names; the results will almost certainly number in the hundreds of thousands.

DJ

EXERCISE

Try searching for a specific tune that you've always wanted and then ripping it with the highest-quality encoding that your computer offers. Then try encoding it at the lowest possible rate and compare the two, noting the difference in sound quality.

DJ

DAY 56

WEEK 8 TEST

Now you know your CD beat matching and mixing tricks, and have entered the domain of digital DJing, take a look at the following questions.

TEST

1 What is an MP3?

2 How much smaller is an MP3 file than a 'normal' version of the same song?

3 What is looping?

4 What is sampling?

5 What is Final Scratch?

6 What is a soundcard?

APPENDIX 1

MUSIC, RECORDS AND MONEY

The starting point here must be to say loud and clear that it's the music that counts, not the format. It don't mean a thing if it ain't got that quantised, mesmerising beat. So, clearly, you need to keep things in perspective and remember that there's no point in changing things at this point if it's at the expense of your hard-learned skills and natural vibe. That said, let's move on.

THOUGHT FOR THE DAY

Every gig is bigger than the sum of its parts.

Most people tend to think that the most important thing to look for when comparing formats is the weight that must be lugged about – and it's true that this is nothing to sniff at; the same number of tunes in a collection will weigh 20 times as much on vinyl as on CD, and both formats are like pure lead compared with the MP3 version of the same collection that can be stored on one CD-ROM (as data) or, even lighter and cheekier, as nothing but an online personalised database that can be accessed from the venue. Such a web-accessed collection is a possibility, but of course it requires that you can get to the site to download the tunes (a risky prospect in even the best of situations). Also, the combination of things that have to all connect and work – PC, web access, modem and so on – makes for a nearly unacceptably nervous arrival at the gig.

Even taking the precaution of phoning ahead to confirm the presence of all the required bits won't necessarily prevent problems, as even a perfectly set-up PC is useless in this situation if the local ISP is down, the phone line is dodgy or, for whatever reason, web access is inconsistent or slow.

The CD option also has its dangers in that fewer clubs have decent CD DJ gear than those with top-flight traditional gear. Again, a call ahead to the club may reassure you that CDs are catered for, but a non-DJ version of a CD player is as bad as no player, so don't forget to ask the model numbers of all the club's players.

Vinyl is obviously still the first choice for over three-quarters of the world's DJs, not least because this format provides the best visual show. Even if you take the (quite legitimate) view that ears matter more than eyes, some clubs have booths that are naturally laid out so as to provide a sort of stage for the DJ, and in this kind of situation it always helps to have big 12" things in your hands.

THE MUSIC

There are many, many different styles and genres of dance music, and new breeds and crossbreeds are being born all the time. Even if you feel dead certain of your life-long dedication to a particular kind of music, there's no harm in checking out new music that you might find interesting, and might find that you wish to experiment with. Virtually every DJ will improve his own mixing and become a better DJ from increasing his awareness of other music. Here's a look at each of the best-known basic genres of dance music.

ACID

The UK dance-music scene had its first big public exposure through the Summers of Love in 1987 and 1988, both of which featured acid house. The sound and the beat feature, as their trademark, the caustic sounds of the Roland TR-303 and TR-808.

AMBIENT

As one of the least formal styles, ambient music is just about anything you care to play, as long as the mix has plenty of space. Beats few and far between – or none at all due to numerous breakdowns – feature prominently between generally mid-tempo or slower grooves.

BIG BEAT

Made internationally commercial through the poppy singles of Fatboy Slim, this music is named after his famous shop in Brighton. The tunes are based on cut-up samples of old-school hip-hop records.

DISCO

The emblem of the '70s continues to permeate dance music, although the original tunes are now often remixed to allow more powerful drum sounds to be inserted, as the old records tend to sound thin and weedy by today's standards.

CRASH COURSE DJ

DRUM 'N' BASS

This is the super-fast (or double-time) breakbeat style that grew out of the early jungle scene. Due to the speed and the frenetic structure of the tunes, it can be one of the more difficult styles to mix, and it certainly keeps you sharp and on your toes.

HARD HOUSE

The natural extension of techno beats with the ravey sounds of house tunes. A less cheesy alternative to house music.

HOUSE

House music is the daddy of modern dance music, as it came from the warehouse parties of Chicago in the immediate post-disco era of the early 1980s. The tunes are almost always vocal and the choruses tend to be quite singalong, which is why house has gained a reputation of cheese and handbags. A disproportionate number of classic dance records are house records, and just about everyone has at least one in their box. As we've seen, it's probably the easiest genre to mix because beginners find the straight four-on-the-floor bass drums easy to pick out.

R&B

This is the fastest-growing genre today, and the tunes are increasingly brilliant. The beats are tricky, however, since they have no easy conventions of bass drums or snares, and a DJ needs to be quite musical to follow the melodies and vocals to mix it.

RAP

Rap has virtually ceased to be definable, as the boundaries are so wide. Old-school rap tends to be unpredictable for mixing, but the new records are without limits.

TECHNO

Probably the most clichéd genre because the beats are so square and the sounds are so apparently unmusical (to a traditionalist's ear). For both reasons, it's a joy to mix – if you can stand the jet engines and chainsaws.

TRANCE

The progressive sound of the early '90s has never stopped sending club-goers into ecstasy. The music has massive ups, huge breakdowns and easy-to-mix beats, and it always carries something of the psychedelic. A recommended (if obvious) choice for beginners to experiment with.

MIXING DIFFERENT STYLES

Mixing different genres together in the same set is a rare undertaking. The conventional wisdom holds that punters come to a club to hear 'their music', and a DJ who plays outside the field is insulting, annoying and breaking the laws on false advertising. (Not to mention the blasphemy of putting the shabbiness and lack of talent of X so close to the brilliance and sheer genius of Y.)

CRASH COURSE DJ

There is an important issue for DJs involved here. Is the DJ's job simply to give the people what they want? Or to challenge the minds and tastes and to broaden the horizons of the masses? To placate or to educate?

The answer lies partly in your personal choice and style; some people see DJing as a job (and may profit handsomely from the conventional business approach) while others see it a mission or something they have to do – and they, too, may profit from the novelty of being unpredictable.

Over the years, there have been many DJs who made themselves self-styled gods through unwavering dedication to a single type of music (Sasha comes to mind). This approach tends to breed a DJ with smoother technique and consistency of quality. The crowds will generally be more loyal (and probably more homogenous) and the DJ is likely to develop more quickly a following of fans that can be trusted to turn out time and time again, even at great distance.

The best DJs of the other extreme (Jeremy Healy is a timeless example) cannot be relied on for anything other than to surprise the crowd and provide a good party atmosphere. The art of mixing different styles right up against each other requires a DJ with excellent skills, adaptability and spontaneity and a very wide knowledge of music. This sort of DJ has the advantage of being able to play anywhere at any time and within any bill, alongside any other DJ. The risk is that, without an easy-to-read label, this DJ is more likely to be left out when a club owner draws up his long-term plan which tries to take in each of the main styles (and corresponding crowds) in turn.

DJ

CHOOSING THE RIGHT RECORD

'Too many DJs perform to themselves.' This is the complaint of club owners, and they probably know best. The complaint mainly refers to DJs who regard their credentials or their dedication to a chosen genre as far more important than the immediate enjoyment of the crowd. The mere fact that, when you finally choose to peer out of the booth and onto the floor, the crowd seem to be dancing is not necessarily proof that you're performing well; the better test relates to the big picture: how was the set as a whole? Did the crowd feel transported?

After you've mastered a few skills and decided on the type(s) of music you want to mix, think about the entire set in one go. Of course, it's vital to leave room to manoeuvre so that you can react to whatever happens on the night, but it's also important to have an overall plan – or at least a vision – of want you want to achieve with a set.

Assuming an average-length set of two hours, imagine a particular club on a night with a particular crowd and start by writing down a hypothetical list of tunes, in the order you might play them, and then consider what you've written. Is there a structure? A set is most memorable if the crowd can identify periods when the tempo or the general vibe made them feel something special – frenzied or excited, relaxed and dreamy, aggressive, fluid, angry, happy, whatever. The perfect set will comprise several moods and move through them slowly enough to make each section distinct and identifiable. Try to create an arc shape to the set where the mood begins in one place, moves through a couple of others and finishes either with the initial feeling or with some kind of resolution.

DJ

Is there enough variation? Decide whether or not you're stretching your own – and the audience's – taste and knowledge. Consider the crowd of the night and compare your list with your estimation of what music they know. Try to pitch your selection just beyond the normal (and boring) limits but without ever going over the top, of course.

Are there sufficient 'moments'? A perfect set needs a few instant highs and lows. The most common methods for creating special moments include big drops and breakdowns, *a cappella* mixes, big recognisable tunes, new tunes with old samples or sounds and high-impact tricks such as stab scratches. Better still, invent new ways to lift the set.

Is there time for you to relax? Nobody can mix long, non-stop sets, hour after hour, night after night, without a few short breaks or some form of stimulant. Think about the points at which you can have a quick break for a drink, a smoke or whatever gets your rocks off in a short time.

Do the timings work? It's all too easy to assume that records are longer than they are. Remember that everything happens quicker than you might think.

Does your set feel right in the cold light of day? Try to remove yourself from that club and consider how you'd view the set the morning after, as the club owner or any reviewer surely will.

EARNING MONEY

The range of earnings for DJs is the length of a piece of string. The top UK DJs will earn tens of thousands for a couple of hours' work (especially on New Year's Eve), while the hardest-working-though-relatively-unknown DJs might, all things considered, end up with less than minimum wage for a long and hard graft.

To add insult to injury, those top geezers might double their income from sales of mix and compilation CDs, record-company consulting and the odd remix. Meanwhile, back on Earth, without becoming a household name you can still turn your mixing into a nice little earner. And it helps to understand how the system works...

The main workplaces for DJs are clubs, bars and mobile-sound-system companies. Clubs are usually the main source, but just how do they make their money? Some mega-clubs (ie Ministry of Sound) have managed to transform themselves into brands and can sell everything from CDs to bars of soap on the strength of the logo, while the vast majority still rely on the punters who show up from night to night.

A club makes its money primarily from the charge on the door and the mark-up on the drinks – although it's impossible to predict which of these will yield more cash. The door money is likely to be split between the owner and the promoter of the night (who was theoretically responsible for bringing the bums through the door), and this split could be in any proportion and could favour either side. The drinks revenue is equally unpredictable; important factors include the size of the bar, the number of bar staff, the nature of the crowd, the time of year and the prices of the drinks.

DJ

The general rule is that a DJ is paid a set fee (negotiated in advance) which will be the lowest figure that the owner – or, more likely, the promoter – can possibly get away with offering. The figure should be based on the scale of the night (the bigger the night, the bigger the pay), but since the DJ is usually left out of the information loop, he has no way of knowing when the figure is out of kilter. Your only weapon here is information, so try as hard as possible to pump the owner, the promoter and anyone else who might be in the know. If you can find anything out, you'll have to do a bit of maths to know if the offered pay is sensible. Multiply the door charge by the expected number of punters and add a few pounds per head for drinks, fags, video games and gambling machines. Take away about 20–40 per cent for the promoter (depending on his professional stature) and a likely sum for rent and insurance (depending on the location of the club) and see how your pay figures against the remainder. If you're ending up with less than ten per cent, you should renegotiate. When playing in bars, much the same formula applies, although it's rare to have a promoter so involved and the drinks revenue is likely to be far higher per head.

Sound-system companies provide DJ entertainment onsite as requested. The highest-paying gigs are usually those where the DJ is hired to play a one-off gig as corporate entertainment or a one-off party such as a wedding. The pay for the DJ can be anything, frankly, and you would need to be able to estimate what the ultimate customer is paying if you wanted to assess your own wage. It's difficult to guess the real figures, but any help you can get from other DJs who may have done these sorts of gigs before will, of course, help.

The important rule that should never be broken is that wages only ever go up, so make sure that each time you play for the same owner/promoter, insist on the biggest rise possible. In some cases, where the club's door charge is relatively low and you're already taking 100 per cent of that take, it might be appropriate to ask for a further percentage (small at first) of the drinks profit, although you should expect heavy resistance when treading on this ground.

ORGANISING YOUR OWN SOUND SYSTEM

The basics of doing it yourself at first seem quite simple, and therefore quite attractive. You hire the gear, set it up and jam. Unfortunately, the small in-between bits are always far bigger than the apparently big bits. The required gear is much the same cast that we've seen before, but with extras:

- the sound system itself (amps, speakers and crossovers);
- the decks (or other players or sources);
- the mixer;
- the required leads;
- lights (for the booth and the floor);
- venue décor (bare breeze blocks all around can be offputting);
- catering (if nothing exists already);
- transport.

The first four items might only be the same gear as you've been using at home, although the speakers will probably need to be bigger, the amps more powerful and the leads much longer.

DJ

If you're staging a gig yourself, it's always easier to find a venue that already has lights, a bar/kitchen and some reasonable decorations. If this is not possible, you would be well advised to leave this to your co-promoter or hire someone else to handle it. Such concerns are too much in addition to everything else.

The key factor to highlight here is the transporting of everything to the gig. Not only does it require a large vehicle, but if you're the only one doing the humping of heavy boxes then think about how this will affect your DJing. Can you do a night's work as the removal man as well as perform properly as the DJ, without dying from exhaustion?

There are, of course, plenty of situations where this is a good option. Providing your own system is often the only possibility for young DJs starting out, and there are many places in the country where no pre-existing suitable venue exists. For many DJs, this is the best and most profitable option, but most find that it's only sustainable if partners can be found (for lighting, transport, and so on).

The other consideration with mobile systems regarding the music is that many customers will be one-off party hosts or 'executive entertainment' chairmen who, you will find, have a very wide range of tastes. For these sorts of gigs, you will need to bring along a few extra records (possibly borrowed from a young sibling or purchased from Woolworths) that don't fit into your usual set.

APPENDIX 2

MARKETING YOURSELF

The most important thing you can do to market yourself is make a demonstration recording of yourself mixing a set. Club owners, promoters, agents, managers and fans will all expect you to have one. Your demo is effectively your business card and it's crucial that it makes the right impression on your behalf. There are several main points to consider when making a demo:

- Choose the right records. Clearly the most important thing your demo says about you is conveyed through the chosen music. Those who listen to your demo will primarily be non-DJs and therefore won't notice the technical aspects and will focus entirely on the tunes. The music needs to reflect the taste of the audience that you're trying to impress.

- Make it the best set you're able to mix. This should be pretty easy as you're under no pressure, no gaze from an audience and you can have as many attempts as you like. Take your own sweet time and get it right.

- Keep it short and sweet. The whole demo should be no more than 90 minutes long.

- Do some market research. Since there is no deadline for delivery, spend a few weeks lending the tape to some key people (trusted mates, other DJs, a club owner) to gather some feedback and, hopefully, constructive criticism.

DJ

- Don't linger on any one record. The audience for your demo won't be dancing; they'll just be listening to see if you've got the talent. Therefore, don't bore them with eight minutes from one record, but rather fly through a lot of records in a relatively short time. Be careful not to go so quickly that you lose the flow, but keep a reasonably rapid pace and make sure the number of records per hour is on the high side.

- Update your mix. Unfortunately, even if you create a set upon which only God himself could improve, you'll have to bin it in a few months and record a whole new one. Don't try to flog a demo full of outdated tunes as it will only prove that you're either out of touch or lazy.

- Think 'substance over style'. Of course it's important that the mixing sounds competent and reasonably professional, but don't get too hung up on getting the entire 90 minutes technically flawless. The person listening to your demo – your prospective employer or manager – isn't concerned with perfection; he just wants to hear evidence that you can keep a crowd happy. So, when you're trying to achieve a balance between a recording of a set with all the right tunes in the right order with a good vibe and one that is technically precise, err of the side of the good tunes. A tiny error here or there will humanise the demo and remind everyone that it was made by a DJ, not a computer

RECORDING YOUR DEMO

The first decision in the demo-making process is whether to record your performance at home or live in the club. For most people, this is an easy decision as they will prefer the more relaxed setting of being at home, but there are those who need the pressure and excitement of an audience to rise to the occasion and do their best work. For these purposes, we'll assume you're working at home, but everything here applies equally in both locations (aside from the second point regarding the connections).

RECORDING MACHINES

There are three choices here: tape recorders, CD recorders or computer-based recording. If tape is your choice, you're likely to be looking at a cassette deck, and while this isn't the best medium, it will suffice. Try to use the best-quality cassette machine and a new tape. There are cassette machines that offer two speeds for recording, and if you can borrow or hire such a machine then you'll find that the faster speed offers superior quality. If not, just get on with it, but pay particular attention to the levels to ensure they are as loud as possible without distorting.

Recordable CD machines are widely available (if expensive) and they are very easy to operate. Just press Record at the right time and make sure the levels are too loud; levels which are too soft might be annoying but won't affect the quality.

The best possible solution is to record the set directly into a computer-based digital-recording/production software system. If your soundcard has no inputs for this, or if you can't purchase or set up a software package yourself, consider finding a friend who will allow you to set your DJ gear up next to his computer for a session. This approach has two main advantages: you don't have to worry about the levels for recording, because they can be changed later; and you can edit your work afterwards by performing two or more separate 'takes' of the set and then later splicing together the best bits from each in order to create one perfect version (which no one could ever guess wasn't performed live as one performance – all pop records are made this way). The disadvantage here is simply that the whole ordeal of computer recording is far more fiddly and a hassle to set up, so it's often quite a pain, but it's nevertheless worth the trouble.

CONNECTIONS

The simplest method for connecting the recording device is by plugging the master outputs of the mixer to the inputs of the recording device. This can be a tricky matter in a club, and you'll probably need to consult the club's techie to be sure that it won't disrupt the sound system. At home, the best idea is to connect the mixer's master outputs (or, better still, the 'record outputs') to the recording device and then the output of the recording device into the amps and speakers. Using this method, you can be sure that you're hearing exactly what's being recorded.

LEVELS

Generally, you need not be too worried about levels because dance music tends to be so loud, without any soft passages (like, say, classical music), that any hiss or noise is unlikely to be noticed. Nevertheless, try to keep the levels on both the mixer and the recording machine at about the oVU mark or just at the beginning of the red area on the meters. Be sure never to let the levels go much above zero, as this may cause distortion. Start by placing the machine in Record and press Pause to monitor the input levels. It is also crucially important – as with all DJing – to keep the volume as consistent as possible so that no section of the set should appear to dip.

PERSONALISING YOUR DEMO

The thing that makes a person buy a product is sometimes called its unique selling point, or USP. A DJ's USP might be his mixing technique, the novelty songs that he mixes in, the genre that he mixes, the combination of genres that he blends into his mix or even his visual style or appearance. Any of these could be the added something that turns the owner, the promoter and the audience into adoring fans and helpful supporters. Whatever your USP might be, it's vital that you convey it in – and on – the demo. Usually, this just means recording your set as best as you can, but keep in mind that the packaging of the demo also serves as your advert and it should have the necessary information on it. This might or might not include a photograph, depending on whether your appearance is part of your USP.

DJ

When you've finished recording (and editing, if possible) your demo, you'll need to copy it for wide distribution. The old method for copying CDs was to pay some sort of professional recording or mastering studio about £10 ($17) per disc for copies, but these day's you'll probably use the CD burner on your computer – or your dad's, if necessary!

Every manufacturer's CD-burning software is slightly different, but the gist of it is that you copy the original CD (the *master*) into the computer's memory and then insert blank recordable CD after blank recordable CD into the burner and hit Record – making sure that you're creating audio CDs and not data CDs.

The most important information, including at least your name and phone number, should go on the CD itself as well as on the case. Once burned, CDs can be labelled with a permanent marker, or a sticker can be stuck on them. (This is a crucial step as most people tend to separate their CDs from their cases soon after the first play and lose the cover or the CD itself.) Remember to include a couple of different contact numbers, as mobiles generally tend to be less permanent than buildings, and if your DJ name isn't your real name, include both.

The outside of the case needs to reflect the kind of DJ that you are, while at the same time stand out among all the hundreds of demos that promoters receive every month. Consider using a bright colour or an unusual pattern on the front and back of the case and especially on the spine as that is what is most often looked at in the CD rack.

Making CD copies of your demo is essential, but it won't help unless you can actually get people to hear it. The most important thing in distributing your demo is to have enough to go around. Don't be stingy when burning CDs – after all, there's no reason to be when blank CDs are available at less than 30p (50¢) each. Whenever you do a gig, make sure you carry at least ten demos with you and hand them out generously to whoever might have even a remote possibility of getting you a gig or in some way helping you in your career.

The most common source for information for clubbers is usually the local press. Think about the publications that you read regularly (to check what DJs are playing where) and try to offer those publications a demo CD together with a flyer for all your gigs. Many newspapers and local magazines have free listings and bulletin-board pages in which you can list your forthcoming appearances, and you should always try to add a sentence or two about your background in order to introduce yourself in the listing, such as 'DJ X, an R&B turntablist who has played throughout London for three years'.

If the chance ever arises to expand the background information that can be printed, have a personal biography on hand and ready to deliver at short notice. Include any interesting details about yourself, but exclude anything that you wouldn't be interested to read about someone else in the same publication.

DJ

Mailing lists are a great source for keeping up with the most recent releases and come with the added bonus of free records. Try sending a weekly chart of your main big tunes to a few music magazines, record companies and promoters; if you persevere, you'll probably find that some will add you to their lists for receiving records and, maybe, even the odd gig.

MANAGERS

It's difficult to find a manager willing to take on a DJ early in his career. They seem to want only those DJs who have already made a name for themselves (and therefore probably don't even need a manager). The truth is – although managers will rarely say this out loud – that managers need to take on unknown DJs, so everyone's got an equal chance in theory, although in practice any added extras like gimmicks or local fan support will improve your chances over a DJ who has 'only talent'. Managers will usually demand about 15–25 per cent of their DJs' booking fees, but this is negotiable and the figure might be higher if the manager can find other opportunities for you to make money. However, it could also be lower if you are helping him to do his work.

Every DJ knows a few horror stories about dishonest managers, and even though most are probably not true you'll need to have a vigilant eye. The best rule to work to is – as with mice in the kitchen – if you think you noticed a problem, you probably did.

If you have aspirations of entering the music business as a producer or artist, finding a manager will be crucial because those sides of the industry will generally deal only with managers. For ordinary DJing, though, you can book all your own gigs just as efficiently as anyone else, even if it is less glamorous.

Agents are really the same beasts as managers except that they group together to form agencies, and so, if signed up to one, you will be part of a bigger stable than you would be with a single manager. This has the advantage of pooling bigger resources, so there are probably more staff and a wider geographic base, but an agency has the disadvantage of size in that you are, to a certain degree, just a number – ie the service is far less personal.

PROMOTERS

Promoters are the angels and the devils of the DJ world. Promoters can make or break a DJ because they wield the power where it counts: locally. You will meet more promoters in your career as a DJ than you can shake a stick at, and your job is to try to separate the good guys from the liars. If a promoter tells you about a new club or a new night that he's setting up that he thinks you're perfect for, be aware of what's going on; even though the promoter may be telling a half-truth (in that he really is involved in an idea for some venue), always remember that promoters are almost certainly telling the same thing to many DJs, and the line could only ever come true if you happened to be in the right place at the right time.

DJ

You can enhance your chances of being in the right place at the right time by appearing enthusiastic and not too cynical, and by doing all the self-marketing suggestions set out above, but keep a foot in the real world and don't ever look desperate and try not to let yourself become emotionally invested in any one hair-brained scheme. All too often, the idea is a pipe dream.

Promoting your own night is also a possibility, although it's a lot more work than just turning up and playing. You'll always need a partner or two to pull off such an ambitious plan, but in a nutshell the main things to consider are:

- **Venue** – You need a suitable place for the night, and probably a licensed one. Consider the capacity and size of the room(s), the ambience, the cost and the hours that it needs to remain open;

- **Sound System** – Most likely, the venue will have its own, but if not, refer to the earlier sections on sound systems;

- **Publicity** – Distributing fliers is the starting point, but you'll need to post many copies and email a catchy version, which are further expenses to consider;

- **DJ** – At least you don't need to spend time on this, as you are now a skilled and competent DJ ready to rock da house.

CONCLUSION

So what now? You've read the book (heard the tunes, worn the T-shirt), practised your arse off and DJ'd through the wee hours for eight whole weeks. But you still aren't Carl Cox. Where's the limo? The freebies? The Lear jet?

This book offered the crash course and you took it. Been there, done that. Now comes the hard part: the long road towards perfection. You might want to read the book *DJ Techniques* (also published by SMT, 2003), which would be an excellent start, and you might even look for someone to give you lessons (Point Blank's DJ school in Hoxton, London, offers a range of excellent courses and tuition and has been voted as having the 'Best Music Production and DJ Courses' by *DJ* magazine in 2002 and 2003).

The most important ingredient, however, is more of the same: practice and more practice. And, to make the elusive quantum leap into professionalism, there's nothing for it but the experience of doing a gig. Get out there. Get gigs. Get DJing.

GLOSSARY

A Cappella

A track containing only vocals (ie no drums, melody or other accompaniment).

Agent

A person (sometimes associated with an agency) who deals with the logistics of DJ bookings, such as sending out demos and press packs, negotiating fees and hotel rooms and arranging flights.

Analogue

Describes a device in which data are represented by voltages which are analogous to the figures they represent. The counterpart of digital.

Anti-skating

A feature on turntables that prevents the needle from skipping across the record.

Bar

A collection of beats, of which there are four per bar in most dance music.

Battle

A DJ competition in which DJs compete against each other in short sets.

Beat Counter

A device on a mixer that counts the beats per minute (bpm) of a track.

BPM

Abbreviation of *beats per minute*, indicating the speed of a track.

Breakdown

The part of a track where the beat slows or stops.

Cartridge

The main bit in the needle where vibrations from the grooves are converted into

an electrical signal.

(Centre) Spindle

The round sticky-up silver bullet that points up from the centre of a deck.

Counterweight

Located at the back of the tone arm and responsible for the amount of pressure

exerted by the needle on a record.

Crossfader

The most important component of the mixer, allowing the DJ to fade between

individual channels or to play two channels simultaneously.

Cue Level

Controls the volume of sound playing through the headphones.

Cue Mix

Enables the DJ to hear what is being played on each channel through the

headphones.

dB

Abbreviation of *decibel*, the unit used to measure volume, or level, of sound.

Digital

Describes data that is stored or transmitted as a sequence of numbers. The

counterpart of analogue.

DJ

Electronica

An American word applied to all dance-music styles.

Gain

The amount by which an amplifier amplifies a signal. (It's what you're turning up when you 'turn it up'.)

Hamster switch

The switch on a mixer that swaps the right channel with the left.

Headshell

Covering that joins directly onto the tone arm, providing a protective housing unit for the cartridge to attach to.

Kill Switch

A switch that instantly cuts one channel's output – or the bass, mid range or treble of a channel – from the mix at a single touch.

Line (Or Aux)

An input socket commonly found on mixers.

Needle

Another word for a *stylus*.

Numark

Manufacturer of DJ equipment such as mixers and turntables.

Outro

End part of a tune.

Pickup Time

The time required for the platter to get up to speed.

Promo

A track that has not been officially released by a record label.

Push Off

To push the record off so that the beats will match with those on another deck

immediately.

RPM

Abbreviation of *revolutions per minute*, usually 33rpm or 45rpm.

Selector (Or Selecta)

Record Selector. A slang term for a DJ.

Slipmat

A circular piece of felt placed between the platter and the record.

Spinback

The practice of stopping a record with the hand and rewinding it quickly.

Stylus

Another word for the needle, the tiny piece of metal that reads the grooves of

the record.

DJ

Target Light

That little pop-up light that shines across the vinyl.

Tempo

Another term for beats per minute (bpm).

Tone Arm

The long, metal arm that is attached at the top-right-hand side of the turntable.

Track

One tune on a record.

Transform

To use a crossfader or a switch to produce a very fast stuttering sound of the tune.

Vestax

One of the leading manufacturers of DJ equipment.

Wax

Slang term for records.

Wheels Of Steel

Slang term for turntables.

White Label

A record that has no information on the label. Generally a promo record.

X-Fader

Shorthand for a crossfader.